Essentials Of Advanced English Grammar

ABOUT THE AUTHOR

Mrs. Ivy Lal is an educationist and has been imparting advanced and higher English education in foreign boards as well as Indian boards for more than 40 years. She has had the privilege of having been tutored by professors like Dr. Ms. Summer Vil, Dr. Ms. Dimit, Ms. Hutchens, Dr. Ms. Shepherd, Ms. Bradly when she was undergoing her graduation at Isabella Thoburn College in 1950s. Her extensive background and knowledge of English grammar has enabled her to bring out this book which is aimed at making one understand and implement grammar better.

Essentials Of Advanced English Grammar

IVY LAL

ZORBA BOOKS

ZORBA BOOKS

Publishing Services in India by Zorba Books, 2019

Website: www.zorbabooks.com
Email: info@zorbabooks.com

Copyright © IVY LAL

ISBN 978-93-88497-81-7
Ebook ISBN 978-93-88497-82-4

All rights reserved. No part of this book may be reproduced or transmitted in any form or by any means, electronic or mechanical, except by a reviewer. The reviewer may quote brief passages,, with attribution, in a review to be printed in a magazine, newspaper, or on the Web—without permission in writing from the copyright owner.

The publisher under the guidance and direction of the author has published the contents in this book, and the publisher takes no responsibility for the contents, its accuracy, completeness, any inconsistencies, or the statements made. The contents of the book do not reflect the opinion of the publisher or the editor. The publisher and editor shall not be liable for any errors, omissions, or the reliability of the contents of the book.

Any perceived slight against any person/s, place or organization is purely unintentional.

Zorba Books Pvt. Ltd.(opc)
Gurgaon, INDIA

INDEX

I	**VERBS**	Page No. 1
	Link verbs	
	Intransitive Verbs	
	Transitive Verbs	
2	**Modal Auxiliary Verbs**	Page No. 8
	Main verbs stand single	
	Verb Need	
3	**Finite and Non Finite Verbs**	Page No. 12
	Finite Verbs	
	Infinitives or Non Finite Verbs	
	Characteristics of infinitives	
4	**Infinitives as Nouns**	Page No. 16
	Infinitives indicate purpose	
5	**Gerunds – Non Finite Verbs**	Page No. 17
6	**Would rather and prefer**	Page No. 26
7	**Had rather and would sooner – than**	Page No. 29
8	**Rather than**	Page No. 30
	Had better	
9	**Present Participle (Non finite verbs)**	Page No. 33
10	**Formation of present participle**	Page No. 35
11	**Present participles used as object pronouns**	Page No. 37
12	**Past Participle**	Page No. 40
13	**+ Perception and – Perception verbs**	Page No. 43
14	**Passive Voice**	Page No. 44
15	**-Perception Verbs**	Page No. 45
16	**Verb Agreement**	Page No. 53
17	**Editing**	Page No. 58
18	**Omitting**	Page No. 66

19	Present Participle and Perfect Participle	Page No. 74
20	Relative Pronouns and Present Participles	Page No. 78
II	**TENSES**	**Page No. 84**
	Simple present	
	Present continuous	
	Negative form	
	Interrogative form	
22	**Action Verbs**	Page No. 88
23	**Past Indefinite or Simple Past Tense**	Page No. 91
24	**Perfect Tense**	Page No. 96
	Present perfect continuous tense	
	Past perfect tense	
	Past perfect continuous tense	
25	**Future Tense**	Page No. 100
III	**MAIN CLAUSE & SUBORDINATE CLAUSES**	**Page No. 107**
27	**Time Clauses with while**	Page No. 111
	In the present time	
	In the past time	
	After and before	
28	**Adverb Phrases of Purpose**	Page No. 116
	Clauses of purpose in the present	
	Purpose clauses in the past	
	Purpose clauses in negative form	
	Purpose clauses with 'lest' and 'for fear'	
29	**Adverb Clauses of Result**	Page No. 121
	Result clauses in the present	
	Result Clause in the past	
	Result clauses with 'such ... that'	
30	**Adverb Clauses of Reason**	Page No. 127
	Participle phrases used instead of reason clauses	
31	**Adjective Clauses**	Page No. 130
	Non – defining or Non-restrictive clauses	

32	Adverb Clauses of Comparison	Page No. 133
33	Noun Clauses	Page No. 136
34	Clauses of Concession or Contrast	Page No. 138
35	Adverb Clauses of Condition or Supposition Permanent truth Unreal condition (imaginary)	Page No. 142
36	Conditional Clauses with Modal Verbs	Page No. 147
37	Connector 'UNLESS' in Conditional Clauses	Page No. 151
38	Reported Speech Direct and Indirect speech Kind of sentences Assertive sentences Interrogative sentences	Page No. 154
39	Imperative Sentences Commands and requests	Page No. 162
40	Exclamations and Wishes Exclamatory sentences	Page No. 164
41	Active and Passive Voice	Page No. 171
42	Direct and Indirect Object	Page No. 178
IV	**CONJUNCTIONS** Co-ordinating Co-relating Subordinating	Page No. 184
44	Clauses of Comparison	Page No. 189
45	Mixed Connectors (Conjunctions)	Page No. 193
V	**ADVERBS** Classification of adverbs Degree Time Frequency Place Quantity Interrogative	Page No. 196

47	Prepositions	Page No. 206
XI	**ARTICLES** Definite	Page No. 219
VII	**DETERMINERS**	
VIII	**ADJECTIVES** Quality Quantity Demonstrative Number Interrogative Degree of comparison	Page No. 232
50	Functional Shift or Nominalisation	Page No. 242
51	Transformation of Sentences	Page No. 244
52	Inversion of Sentences	Page No. 259
53	Question Tags	Page No. 262
54	Adjectives as Plural Nouns	Page No. 264
IX	**ADJECTIVES AS NOUNS**	Page No. 266
56	Prefixes Suffixes	Page No. 267
X	**COMPREHENSION PASSAGES** Climate Change – A myth or a Reality Is Digital Equity a Reality A Dusty Airport	 Page No. 275 Page No. 281 Page No. 285
XI	**POEMS** Money Plant A Traveler of Life To Kiss The Stars Freedom	 Page No. 288 Page No. 291 Page No. 294 Page No. 296

PREFACE

The book is designed specially to simplify the complicated arena of grammatical structures from simple to complicated ones, followed by practice exercises required by any board examination. It is a complete package of advanced English grammar. A few comprehension passages and poems are also given to check the readers' comprehension and vocabulary capacity.

Dear Readers

I am happy to present this book to my readers which will enable them to understand English grammar in the best possible way. This book is the result of my mastery in English enforced with more than four decades of being an educationist in advanced and higher education in Foreign boards as well as Indian boards of education.

This book is for all those who are keen to go ahead in life with a bright future which comes through speaking and writing a language correctly. There are many languages spoken all over the world even the tribal languages are there. Since all the languages can't be learnt by all, the English language has been taken as a universal language of communication so that we all are connected and feel as a family and exchange our ideas. Learning any language is not difficult until and unless it is simplified for a student to understand and implement it in daily, professional as well as personal life.

This book has plenty of practice exercises in grammar and has clarified some ambiguities in the transitive verbs, intransitive and link verbs. You will understand them easily so grammar won't be any more complicated for you. Besides grammar basics, this book helps the reader to communicate in emphatic, interesting and expressive manner. Section entitled 'Transformation of Sentences' does the same, as if clauses c.

This book is aimed for class studies and self study. It provides the best platform for understanding complex English. It is the best book that can be inducted in the International board, CBSE, ICSE and others. It not only simplifies and strengthens a high school student's knowledge of English but also those who are preparing for advanced English language competitions, interviews, brushing up their grammar, or teachers who need a reference book.

May my readers climb high up like eagles with their Wings!

Author – Mrs. IVY Lal

author.ivylal@gmail.com

ACKNOWLEDGMENT

I am thankful to my children and grand-children for having supported me to accomplish my aspiration of sharing my knowledge of English Grammar through a book. My elder son, Rodrick Rajive Lal – an educationist, a writer, author, poet and a vivid blogger has not only enabled me in shaping this book but has also contributed passages and poems. Having already published four books, his insight and knowledge has enabled me to sail through the process of getting this book published. My younger son, Sanjay Iwrin Lal has helped me edit and compile the numerous pages through hours we sat together. I am also thankful to my grand-daughters, Aastha, Ekta & Rhea for assisting me to type certain pages. Though they were teenagers and preoccupied with their studies yet they didn't shirk from helping me. May God bless you! I also thank my daughters-in-law, Nidhi and Sapna, my daughter Enid Madhu for being my well-wishers and encouraging me. My younger grand children, Raima, Aadi and Nimishia for enabling me to write the manuscript undisturbed. I am also thankful to my publisher – Zorba Books Pvt. Ltd. (opc) who stood by me in giving the final shape and bringing it to you. A special thanks to Sunil Atri of Zorba Books for keeping a close follow up and enabling this book take its final form.

VERBS

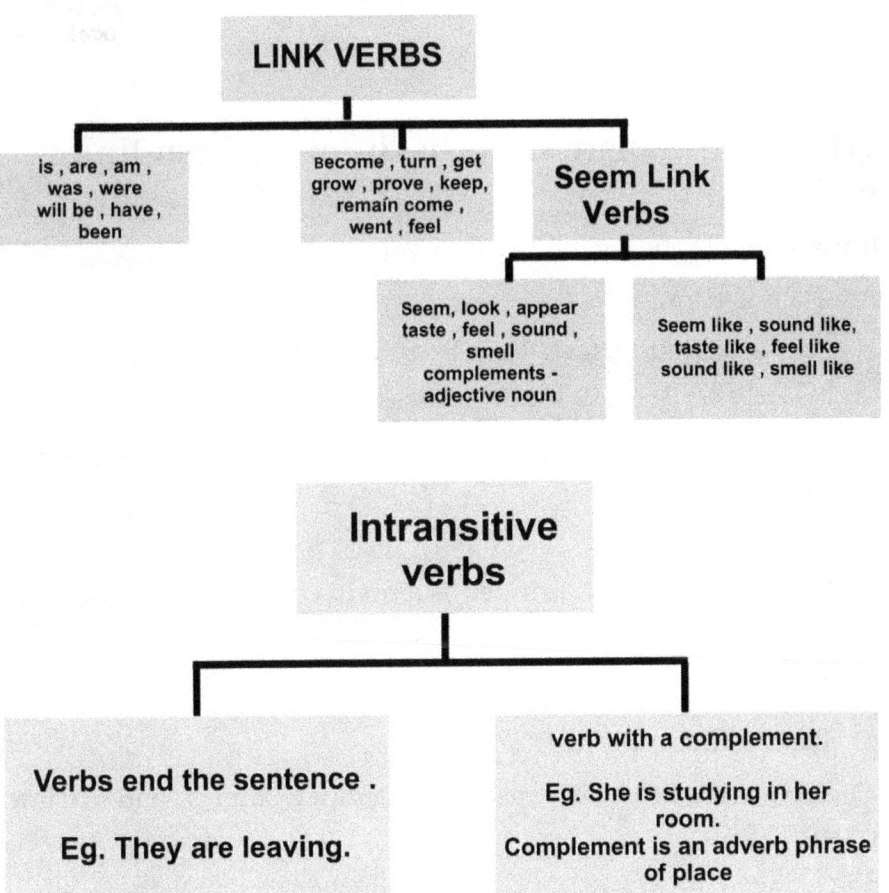

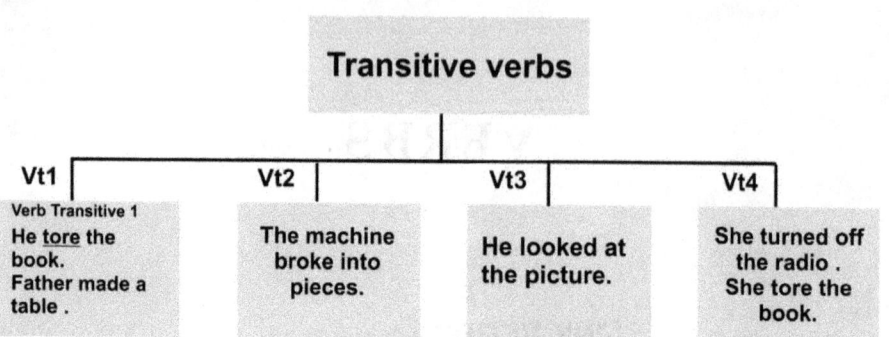

Why are intransitive verbs different from link verbs?

Intransitive verbs can end with a verb.

As- Raju is running.

Raju is running fast. Fast is an adverb complementing the verb running.

Whereas, link verbs can't end the sentence without a complement.

As- Ranjita is. (wrong)

Ranjita is a singer. 'a singer' is a noun complement. It helps to complete the sentence.

Thomas became. (wrong)

Thomas became a doctor.

Both intransitive and link verbs cannot change a sentence into passive voice.

As- The teacher is teaching. It can't have passive voice.

Is teaching – intransitive verb

The teacher is teaching the class. Is teaching- transitive verb

Passive voice- The class is being taught by the teacher.

Link verb- Sohan has become a pilot.

VERBS

Passive voice- a pilot has become by Sohan. (wrong)

Note- A list of link verbs is given on page 1.

A. Exercise

Underline the verbs and write what type they are- intransitive, link verb or transitive verb.

1) Rain ended the match.
2) Mr. Roy was a painter.
3) A strong wind was blowing.
4) I felt hungry.
5) He looks ill.
6) Father asked the son a question.
7) The baby broke the feeding bottle.
8) The woman was gathering dry twigs.
9) The runners are running.
10) The milk has turned sour.
11) The Narayens always compete with others.
12) The tailor closes the shop at 8 o'clock.
13) My son gave up smoking.
14) We are going out.
15) They are going out to attend a wedding.
16) The guard blew the whistle.
17) The child has broken one of my cups.
18) Mr. Mal's son appears sick.
19) This fruit tastes bitter.
20) You can remain with us.
21) The doctor has gone home.

22) It smells like rose perfume.
23) You must throw the garbage in the garbage bin.
24) The board appointed Mr. Ranjit as a manager.
25) Students are studying.
26) Students are studying in different rooms.
27) I am a teacher.
28) You are a business man.
29) The plumber hasn't done proper work.
30) Avocado tastes like butter.

Transitive Verbs

Note

a) The sentences with transitive verbs always have an object so they can be changed into passive voice. As- the baby **broke a cup**.

b) Some sentences have a preposition before a noun. As- The chief guest looked at the pictures.

B Exercise

Change the following sentences into passive voice.

1) The woman was gathering twigs.
2) Raj closes the shop at eight.
3) They have blown off the bridge.
4) They brought us some furniture.
5) Uncle bought some interesting puzzles for us.
6) He gave up smoking.
7) She has broken off her engagement.

VERBS

8) The captain ordered the soldier to stand in a single file.
9) The guard blew the whistle and waved the green flag.
10) Our aunt told us to choose any gift displayed on the table.

C Exercise

Choose the correct meaning for the given sentence.

1) I caught him eating jam.
    a) He was caught to eat jam.
    b) He was caught while he was eating jam.
2) One of the invigilators found her while she was cheating in the exam.
    a) One of the invigilators found her cheating in the exam.
    b) One of the invigilators found her to cheat in the exam.
3) The farmer left the boy threshing the grain.
    a) The farmer left the boy to thresh the grain.
    b) The farmer left the boy while he was threshing the grain.
4) We left John arranging the books on shelves.
    a) John was left to arrange the books on shelves.
    b) When we left John, he was arranging books on the shelves.
5) The police caught the thief breaking the safe.
    a) The police saw the thief and caught him while he was breaking the safe.
    b) The police caught him to break the safe.

6) You can leave the child to play with these children.
   a) You can leave the child so that he can play with the children.
   b) You can leave the child to play.
7) The police recognized the thief climbing up the ladder.
   a) The police recognized the thief while he was climbing up the ladder.
   b) The police caught the thief to climb up the ladder.
8) Malini watched the cat stealing silently towards the mouse.
   a) Malini watched the cat while it was stealing towards the mouse.
   b) Malini watched the cat so that it might steal towards the mouse.

Some transitive verbs have direct and indirect objects. These objects can change their places using 'to' or 'for'.

Example - He gave me a book.
<u>Book</u> is a direct object.
<u>Me</u> is an indirect object.
Changing places of objects will take 'to'
He gave a book to me.
Use 'for' to change the places of direct and indirect objects.

Example - Father made her a swing.
A swing- direct object
Her- indirect object
Father made a <u>swing</u> for <u>her</u>.

VERBS

Exercise

Rewrite the following sentences changing the places of direct and indirect objects. Use correct preposition. Use 'to' for group A and 'for' for group B.

A

1) Have they paid you the money?
2) Please lend me some of your Physics books.
3) Your uncle handed her a bag.
4) Grandmother told her grand-son a story.
5) Charu's mother read her a letter.
6) Will you please throw me the ball?
7) Can you give me proper advice?
8) My aunt denies me nothing.

B

1) Will you do me a favour?
2) Can you get me some fresh roses?
3) She ordered us a cake.
4) Did you leave him any sandwiches?
5) He told me that he will buy her some stationery.
6) Can you spare me some of your time?
7) My father bought his brother a new car.
8) He left her a box of chocolates.

Edit the following sentences. Write the wrong word then write the correct word beside it.

My friend gave a book with me.	a) _____
I was thankful to her.	b) _____

As she is going back					c) _____
home, she fall down					d) _____
and was seriously injure.				e) _____
Her mother get very upset.				f) _____
There was no one to help her.			g) _____

Yesterday Sonu leave his				a) _____
father getting ready to went			b) _____
to his field. Today he have				c) _____
given me the news of his successful.	d) _____
I am anxious to reached home			e) _____
As soon as it was possible.				f) _____

One word is missing. Write the missing word between two words it should be.

It looks an orange.						a) _____
I feel eating it.							b) _____
But my friends are advising				c) _____
not to eat it. Have listened to them.	d) _____
We are good friends we					e) _____
Protect each other.						f) _____

We looked back saw our					a) _____
teacher behind. She came				b) _____
towards us told us						c) _____
the trip to Nainital.						d) _____
We started jump							e) _____
made a great noise						f) _____

Modal Auxiliary Verbs

Modal auxiliary verbs help the main verb to take its tense and express the mood or mode of the main verb.

VERBS

There are 'be' verbs is, are, am, was, were, has, have, do, shall, will, can, may, must, ought to, dare, used to

A. Exercise

Fill in the blanks using 'be' verbs, have or do.

1) They _____ going now.
2) He _____ playing outside when I passed by his house.
3) The typist _____ done his work.
4) Please _____ (not do) disturb me.
5) The farmer _____ (not do) need to come home through the forest.

Use modal verbs as modal auxiliary verbs take place before the main verb.

Shall, will, should, would, can, may, might, must, ought to, dare, need, used to.

1) I <u>Shall</u> (see) them tomorrow.
2) We _____ (plough) the field as soon as it is possible.
3) Naina _____ take a blanket with her.
4) Father _____ advise me when I was a child.
5) Rohan _____ see the doctor as he feels sick.
6) They _____ fetch us some fresh eggs.
7) The guard _____ (not do) do his duty seriously.
8) 'B' team _____ win the game as their scores are going higher and higher.
9) When Manoj was in class 10, he _____ buy a bottle of Coca Cola from this shop.
10) The short boy _____ jump over the fence.
11) Students _____ not miss classes as attendance is compulsory.

12) Mohan _____ not come near the cobra.
13) Need she _____ (work, works) so hard?
14) If the workers _____ (doesn't, don't) come on time, they _____ (be) marked absent.
15) We _____ respect our elders.

Main Verbs Stand Single

Verbs used as main verbs without another verb are single. Use the following verbs to fill in the blanks: is, am, are, was, were, has, have, need.

B. Exercise

Fill in the blanks with main verbs given above.

1) During those days, they _____ (be) happy.
2) She _____ (need) some more time.
3) Singhs _____ (be) decent people.
4) Neither pen _____ (has, have) ink.
5) Rana _____ (be) absent yesterday.
6) Both the students _____ (has, have) capabilities.
7) Each of the students _____ (has, have) enough stationery.
8) This food ____ (be) enough for four people.
9) I _____ (be) a brave man.
10) Not only Neetu but also Rajini _____ (has, have) beautiful dresses.

Verb Need

When the verb 'need' is used as need not or needn't. Follow the following structures-

VERBS

1) He needs not leave so early. (WRONG)
   He need not leave so early. (RIGHT)
2) She needn't to exert herself. (WRONG)
   She needn't exert herself. (RIGHT)
3) Needs he take transfer? (WRONG)
   Need he take transfer? (RIGHT)
4) Need he to take transfer? (WRONG)
   Need he take transfer? (RIGHT)

Note- The verb 'dare' also follows the same structures as 'need'.

When the verb 'need' or 'dare' take a helping verb, they are used in usual, normal way.

Example - He does not dare to take this challenge.
Does he dare to take this challenge?
She does not need to give an elaborate explanation.
Do they need to buy all the books?

Edit the following sentences. write the incorrect word in the first blank and the correct one in the second blank.

She needs not stay back   a) _____ _____
as she have no other work.   b) _____ _____
She can came tomorrow   c) _____ _____
a little later as she need   d) _____ _____
some rest. She is an eficient   e) _____ _____
Workers.   f) _____ _____

The volunteers may comes   a) _____ _____
On time. He will sorts out   b) _____ _____
The books and lays them   c) _____ _____

On there respective shelves.   d) _____
The librarian will   e) _____
also helped them   f) _____

Write the missing word which should be between two correct words.

The doctor done the surgery.   a) _____
He is expert surgeon.   b) _____
All of his surgeries given   c) _____
the best results. Patients all   d) _____
Over India come him.   e) _____
He always a smiling face   f) _____
which makes patients fearless   g) _____

The police do their best   a) _____
guard this place   b) _____
thieves, gangsters, chain   c) _____
snatchers, drunkards.   d) _____
People want live in   e) _____
peaceful surroundings.   f) _____

Finite and Non – Finite Verbs
Finite Verbs
A finite verb is a verb without which a sentence can't be made.

Example :
    She went out to collect the letters.
    'went' is a finite verb without which this sentence can't be made.

VERBS

'to collect' cannot form a sentence without the verb 'went'(finite verb).

We are <u>going shopping</u>.

'are' is a finite verb, the basic factor of this sentence.

'going' or 'shopping' can't make the sentence without the finite verb 'are.'

Note :

When used in present tense, their structure change according to singular/plural subject. They may take an 's' or without an 's.'

In simple past tense 'was' may change into 'were' or vis-a-vis.

Example:

Mrs. Kumar teache<u>s</u> English.

Mrs. Kumar and Mrs. Das <u>teach</u> English.

I <u>am</u> a business man.

You <u>are</u> a business man.

This child <u>has</u> many toys.

These children <u>have</u> many toys.

She <u>does</u> hard work.

Labourers <u>do</u> hard work.

Yesterday Rohan and his friend <u>were</u> absent.

Last Monday Richard <u>was</u> absent.

The underlined words given above are finite verbs; they have incurred changes according to their singular or plural form of verbs. They are in simple present tense except 'was' and 'were.'

Infinitives or Non-Finite Verbs

Infinitives have the character of a verb as well as of a noun.

Example :

She likes <u>to swim</u>.

'to swim' indicates an action so it shows its verbal quality. It is also acting like a noun complement. So we can say, infinitives are verbal nouns.

Characteristics of Infinitives

A. Infinitives can be part of a sentence but they cannot make a complete sentence without a finite verb.

Example :

    We <u>have to look</u> into the matter.

    A Finite verb is 'have.'

    Infinitive is 'to look'

    I saw him <u>pass</u> by my house.

    Finite verb 'saw'

    Infinitive 'pass'

    This sentence can't be constructed without the finite verb 'saw.'

B. Some infinitives are without 'to.'

Example :

    He will <u>come</u> tomorrow.

    She must <u>reveal</u> the truth.

    Underlined words are infinitives without 'to.'

    The infinitives that come after the following verbs do not take 'to.'

    These verbs or expressions are shall, will, do, did, should, would, may, might, must, can, could, had better, had rather, would rather, sooner than, rather than, let, see, hear and make when they are used in active voice.

    Need not, dare not, don't take 'to' after them

VERBS

Exercise 1

Complete the following sentences with infinitives according to the instructions given in 'B.'

1. Let him _____.
2. I will not let you _____.
3. The boss made him _____.
4. All of you need not _____.
5. He daren't _____.
6. Some of us heard _____.
7. The students had better _____.
8. The musician would rather _____.
9. I had rather _____ than _____.
10. My friend would rather _____.

C. Some infinitives take 'to' before them.

The given verbs are commonly followed by infinitive with 'to.'

Learn, refuse, hesitate, remembered (past tense), regret, decide, neglect, determine, promise, propose, prepare, forget (simple/ simple past tense) attempt, undertake, swear, fail, manage, consent, care, want (with/without an object).

Exercise 2

Answer the following questions using the verbs given beside each question.

1. Why is he going to this institution? (learn, because)
2. What do you want to do? (decide)
3. What directions do the students have to follow to do this exercise? (attempt)
4. Why has she borrowed your bike? (want)

5. Why has this business man failed in his business? (manage)
6. Why didn't you bring our clothes from the drycleaner? (forget)
7. Before attempting an interview what does a candidate have to do / (prepare)
8. Why do you have to become so serious? (undertake, because)

1. Infinitives as nouns

An infinitive does the work of a noun if it works like a subject, object after the verb, object of a preposition or as a complement.

Example 1

(a) <u>To err</u> is human.

To err – subject (noun)

(b) I want <u>to read</u> this book.

To read – object (noun)

(c) She likes <u>to sing</u>.

To sing – noun complement to the verb 'likes.'

(d) The clock is about <u>to fall</u>.

To fall – object to preposition 'about.'

2. Infinitives indicate purpose

(a) They decorated the hall <u>to welcome</u> the guests.

To welcome – purpose

Exercise 2

Join the following sentences using infinitive with 'to.'

Example: Q. The teacher will be there. she will make the arrangements for the party.

Ans. The teacher will be there <u>to make</u> arrangements for the party.

1. Mother has to stay back. she must take care of the baby.
2. You must leave early. Then only you will catch the train.
3. He didn't have money. he couldn't send his son to school.
4. Eat balanced diet. you will be healthy.
5. Some thieves followed him. They took away his money.
6. He is ashamed. He is humiliated.
7. The police should arrest the criminal. The criminal should stop committing crimes any further.
8. We must earn. We must survive.
9. The boy has climbed up the tree. He want to pick some mangoes.
10. Mother doesn't allow her daughter to eat more than needed. She wants to prevent her from becoming obese.

Gerunds - Non Finite Verbs

Infinitives and gerunds are verbal nouns. Gerunds are – ing form of verbs.

Functions Of Gerunds

A. A gerund works like subject of a sentence.

   Example

   Running is a good exercise.

   Running – subject – it is a noun

B. A gerund is placed after a verb; it works like an object of that verb.

   Example

   Children like <u>playing</u> outdoor games.
   Playing – object to the verb 'like' (noun).
   A word that works like object to a verb is a noun.

C. The greatest need of the hour is <u>controlling</u> the growth of population.

   Controlling – noun complement

   It is clear that gerunds work like noun complements as well.

D. If an -ing form of a verb is placed after a preposition, it works like an object to that preposition.

   Example

   Gandhi ji believed that we had to get independence <u>by fighting without shedding blood.</u>
   'Fighting' is object to the preposition 'by'
   'shedding' is the object of the preposition 'without'
   Because of their structural construction, shedding and fighting are gerunds, working like nouns.

E. An answer to 'what' is always a noun.

   Example

   The <u>teaching</u> of a language is a skill.
   Q. What is a skill?
   Ans. Teaching of a language.
   Since 'teaching' is the answer to the question 'what', it is a noun.

F. A possessive adjective tells something about a noun likewise possessive adjective tells something about a gerund.

   Example

   I gave him <u>my</u> book.
   'my' – possessive adjective
   'book' – noun
   <u>My revealing</u> the truth, solved the problem.
   'My' – possessive adjective
   'revealing' – gerund

Note :

   -ing form used after the following possessive adjectives is a gerund.

   $\left.\begin{array}{l} \text{My} \\ \text{Your} \\ \text{His} \\ \text{Our} \\ \text{Its} \\ \text{Their} \\ \text{Her} \end{array}\right\}$ + -ing forms are gerunds

G. A gerund along with a noun works as an object.

   Example

   (a) This is my father's walking stick.
   'walking' – gerund
   'stick' - noun
   Walking stick means father's stick for walking.
   The hidden preposition 'for' indicates that walking is the object to the preposition 'for', hence it is a gerund.

H. The meaning of a sentence changes when a gerund is used in active or passive voice.

Example

(a) The king loved to praise others. Active voice

Means – whenever the King noticed that somebody had done something praiseworthy, he praised him happily.

(b) The king loved being praised. Passive voice

Means – the King wanted people to praise him. It gave him happiness.

Note that the meanings of sentence a and b have changed because of the change in their voices.

I. In order to give emphasis that an action took place in the past, simple gerund can be changed into perfect gerund.

Example

The inspector denied receiving a bribe.

'receiving' – simple gerund

The inspector denied having received a bribe.

'having received' – perfect gerund, giving emphasis to the fact that the bribe was not received in the past.

J. When an incident happened in the past, but is remembered now at the time of speaking, -ing form (gerund) is used after the verb remember.

Example

I remember meeting him ten years ago.

Means – I met him ten years ago but I am speaking about that meeting now.

The following verbs take –ing forms (gerunds) after them

Avoid, finish, deny, suggest, dread, risk, delay, keep, detest, miss, involve, save (save oneself the trouble of), recollect, admit, imagine (objection), prevent, consider, enjoy, postpone, stop, can't stand (can't tolerate or endure) can't help (can't prevent or avoid), no use, no good, worth

Example

  I avoid taking interest in their jokes.

  'Avoid' - verb

  'taking' – gerund

  Gerund is placed after the verb avoid.

K. I am interested in collecting foreign stamps.

 'in' – preposition

 'collecting' – gerund object to the preposition 'in'.

Exercise 1

Fill in the blanks with suitable gerunds according to the structures given in A, B, C, D, E & F

Example:

<u>Walking</u> is a good exercise

 1. _____ does harm the body. (smoke)

 2. Seeing is _____. (belief)

 3. He was imprisoned for _____ a bribe.

 4. Sam enjoys _____ in his bath.

 5. He sat down for his breakfast after _____ his hands.

6. John is an expert in _____ wild elephants.
7. I don't like his _____ all the time.
8. One of his hobbies is _____.
9. People hate _____ at bus stop.
10. They conducted a camp for _____ the young cricketers.
11. _____ in buses is prohibited.
12. The director will take their _____ over the school fence as an offense.
13. Stop _____.
14. He can't help _____ even though his health is ruined.

Exercise 2

Rewrite the following sentences using gerunds according to the structures given in the groups G & H.

Example

Q.   You can buy these <u>desks for writing.</u>

Ans.   You can buy these <u>writing desks.</u>

1. They gave us some tools for digging.
2. We have bought a machine for washing.
3. She is asking for a brush for painting.
4. They have bought a bicycle for racing.
5. The minister didn't like people flattering him.
6. Nobody likes to be abused.
7. The painter loves admiration for his paintings.
8. He hates to be left all alone.
9. Children dislike to be checked while playing.

VERBS

Exercise 3

Rewrite the following sentences according to the structures given in group 'I'; use perfect gerunds.

Example

Q. The boy admitted skipping one of the classes.
Ans. The boy admitted having skipped one of the classes.

1. He is sorry for doing such a thing.
2. The police accused him of stealing the grain.
3. I recollect looking at my watch just before I left home.
4. The teacher can't imagine your behaving in such a manner.
5. Mother didn't mind his joining the cricket team.
6. I don't remember your saying so.
7. Do you repent of taking up that job?
8. They are contented because they achieved their goals.
9. Will they remember their objecting to the proposal.

Exercise 4

Join the following pairs of sentences using a gerund as object to a preposition.

List of prepositions – to, with, of, on, without, in, before, for, from, by, instead of, after

Example

Q. The thief entered the house. He broke a window.
Ans. The thief entered the house by breaking the window.

1. Teachers congratulated the school team. The team won the football match.
2. I won't excuse you. You should take the examination.

3. We must breathe. We can't live.
4. They locked the door. They went out.
5. The magistrate fined the cyclist. He cycled at night without a lamp.
6. He reads poetry. He finds great pleasure in it.
7. He wants to catch fish. He doesn't want to wet his hands.
8. He sleeps in the open. He is used to it.
9. Stephan wants to pass the exam. He has set his mind on it.
10. The boys took their positions on the field. They had every hope to win.
11. That visiting guest was eating fish every day. He was fed up.
12. The woodcutter is tired. He cut the trees the whole day.

Exercise 5

Complete the following sentences using gerunds. You can take help from the words given in brackets and any other if needed.

1. It's no use _____ in the mud (spoil).
2. We're going _____ (fish).
3. It's no good _____ (marriage, delay).
4. They spend hours _____ (discuss).
5. He succeeded _____ (climb).
6. She insisted _____ (type).
7. He was accused _____ (grain, steal).
8. These people are looking forward _____ (abroad, go).
9. John is used to _____ (cold climate, live).

10. Our friends aren't accustomed _____ (hot food, eat).
11. The villagers accused the stranger _____ (destroy, site).
12. The daughter is thinking _____ (drive, learn).
13. Aunt has no objection _____ (what you have to say, hear).
14. These students aren't used to _____ (pronounce) this word correctly.
15. I can't help _____ (pity) those wounded soldiers.
16. This material isn't worth _____ (buy).
17. The examination committee may postpone _____ (hold) the meeting.
18. Has she finished _____ (cook) food.
19. The guard kept _____ (watch) the figure moving in the courtyard.
20. Tom doesn't dread _____ (head, step, cobra).

Some verbs can take both an infinitive or a gerund after them.

Exercise 6

Join the following sentences in two ways using a gerund and then an infinitive.

Example

The children have gone out. They will play.

Ans. The children have gone out for playing.

      The children have gone out to play.

1. The chief has taken him. He will investigate the crime.
2. The nurse has taken the syringe. She will inject the patient.
3. The maid needs a duster. She will clean the table.
4. The committee has been set. The committee will take the decision.
5. I have noted down your complaints. The complaints will be presented in the meeting.
6. I will study the chapters thoroughly. I will rank the first among student all the sections of class eleven.
7. Sunita goes swimming everyday. She will reduce her weight.
8. The labourers are drinking sufficient water. They want to prevent themselves from getting dehydrated.

Would rather and prefer

Would rather and prefer indicate more liking for something.

Exercise 7
Example
I like to eat mangoes. I don't like to eat bananas.

    A. I prefer eating mangoes to eating bananas.
    B. I prefer mangoes to bananas.
    C. I would rather eat mangoes than bananas.

Structures for the sentences given above. Use any two structures.

    Like _____ to eat (infinitive with to).
    Prefer _____ eating (gerund).
    Prefer _____ mangoes (noun object).
    Would rather _____ eat (infinitive without to).

Join the following sentences using **'prefer'** and then **'would rather'**.

1. She likes to read novels. She doesn't like to read poetry.
2. Children like to play outdoor games. They don't like to play indoor games.
3. Rani likes to eat chocolate. She doesn't like to eat biscuits.
4. I like to stitch dresses. I don't like to stitch men's suits.
5. Abdul likes to work in a watch shop. He does like to work in a grocery shop.
6. My friend likes to wear studded jewelry. She doesn't like to wear plain jewelry.
7. Mrs. Anjali likes to teach lower grades. She doesn't like to teach higher grades.
8. Tom likes to climb up towering mountains. He doesn't like to climb low plateaus.
9. In summers students like to attend morning classes. They don't like to attend afternoon classes.

Would rather showing past preferences
Structure
Would rather + have + past participle

Exercise 8
Rewrite the following sentences showing past preferences

Example
I wanted to visit Switzerland but I had to visit Romania.

Ans. I would rather have visited Switzerland than Romania.

1. Mrs. Jenny wanted to write novels but she had to write short stories.

2. They wanted to swim in a lake but they had to swim in a pool.
3. The travelers wanted to take a shortcut route but they had to take a longer one.
4. We wanted to pluck red roses but we had to pluck white ones.
5. I wanted to buy sweets but I had to buy fruits.
6. We wanted to stop at lake Abyata but we had to stop at lake Chamo.
7. They wanted to fly via London but they had to fly via Paris.
8. Maria wanted to ride a Horse but she had to ride a Pony.
9. These students wanted to carry some books to the library but they had to carry chairs.
10. The staff wanted to enjoy their holiday but they had to go to office for an urgent meeting.

Would rather shows a particular choice of a person.
Exercise 9

Structure

Noun + would rather + noun + simple past tense

Example

My mother wants me to eat fruit instead of sweets.

Ans. My mother would rather I ate fruit than sweets.

Join the following sentences according to the example given above.

1. Helen wants her friend go for higher studies instead of taking up a job.
2. Father wants his son watched knowledgeable serials instead of whiling away his time.

3. The teacher wants her students get A's instead of B's.
4. The doctor wants the patient to take more rest instead of exerting himself.
5. Father wants me to go abroad than stay in India.
6. Sheila's uncle wants her to study medicine than engineering.
7. The shopkeeper wants the customer to buy the old stuff instead of the new stuff.
8. Grand-mother wants Rashmi to stay with her
9. My parents want my brother to take medicines regularly.
10. The monitor wants the class to keep quiet.

Had rather and would sooner - - - than

Note : would rather, prefer, had rather, would sooner - - - than, the given expressions mean preference, choice, liking.

Exercise 10

Rewrite the following sentences using 'had rather and would sooner – than.

Example

I prefer playing to working

Ans. I had rather play than work.

   I would sooner play than work.

1. The patient dying to suffering so.
2. Our family prefers traveling by air than by water.
3. This organization prefers helping the underprivileged to helping the privileged ones.
4. God prefers redeeming the poor with humble heart and contrite spirit to the bragging rich.
5. She prefers putting in more effort to succeed lying lazily.

Rather than

Rather than shows choice.

Example

Rather than being rude to the authorities, he humbled himself.

Ans.   Instead of being rude to the authority, he humbled himself.

Exercise 11

1. Rather than telling a lie, he risked imprisonment.
2. Rather than disturbing the party, he left the hall quietly.
3. Rather than showing his anger, he started to play the organ.
4. Rather than whiling away his time, he started writing books.
5. Rather than eating two day old food from the fridge, he prepared a fresh meal.

Had better

Had better means should or ought to.

Exercise 12

Rewrite the following sentences using 'had better'.

Example

We ought to take care of our pets.

Ans.   We had better take care of our pets.

1. She ought to put on her coat if she is feeling cold.
2. These children should not play in front of the principal's office.
3. The patient should not stop the treatment.
4. You ought not to buy this car.

VERBS

5. We should work hard if we want good results.
6. They ought to tell the truth if they want to escape the punishment.
7. You should be physically and mentally fit for this job.
8. The teacher should take clearance from the school if he wants to join another school.

Answers of exercise
Exercise 1

1.	Smoking	2.	Believing	3.	Taking
4.	Singing	5.	Washing	6.	Training
7.	Talking	8.	Hunting	9.	Waiting
10.	Training	11.	Smoking	12.	Jumping
13.	Shouting	14.	Smoking		

Exercise 2

1. They gave us some digging tools.
2. We have bought a washing machine.
3. She is asking for a painting brush.
4. They have bought a racing bicycle.
5. The minister didn't like flattering people.
6. Nobody likes being abused.
7. The painter loves being admired for his paintings.
8. He hates being left alone.
9. Children dislike being checked while playing.

Exercise 3

1. He is sorry for having done such a thing.
2. The police accused him of having stolen the grain.

3. I recollect having looked at my watch before I left home.
4. The teacher can't imagine your having behaved in such a manner.
5. Mother didn't mind his having joined the cricket team.
6. I don't remember your having said so.
7. Do you repent of having taken up that job?
8. Having achieved their goals, they are contented.
9. Will they remember having objected to their proposal.

Exercise 4

1. Teachers congratulated the school team on winning the football match.
2. I won't excuse you from taking the exam.
3. We can't live without breathing.
4. They went out after locking the door.
5. The magistrate fined the cyclist for cycling at night without a lamp.
6. He reads poetry for getting pleasure from it.
7. He wants to catch fish without wetting his hands.
8. He is used to sleeping in the open.
9. Stephan has set his mind on passing the exam.
10. The boys had every hope of winning the match.
11. That visiting guest was fed up with eating fish every day.

Exercise 5

1. It is no use spoiling this dress.
2. We are going fishing.
3. It is no good delaying the marriage.
4. They spent hours discussing the issue.

5. He succeeded in climbing up the peak.
6. She insisted on typing that letter.
7. He was accused of stealing the grain.
8. These people are looking forward to going abroad.
9. John is used to living in cold climate.
10. Our friends aren't accustomed to eating hot food.
11. The villagers accused the stranger of destroying the site.
12. My daughter is thinking of learning driving.
13. Aunt has no objection to hearing to what you have to say.
14. These students aren't used to pronouncing certain words correctly.
15. I can't help pitying those wounded soldiers.
16. This material isn't worth buying.
17. The examination committee may postpone holding the exams.
18. Has she finished cooking?
19. The guard kept watching the figure.
20. Tom doesn't dread stepping the head of the cobra.

Present Participle (non finite verbs)

Present participle is an ing form of a verb. It is a verbal adjective as it has the quality of a verb as well as an adjective.

Present Participle can work in the following ways

A) Present participle qualifies a noun; it can be placed before a noun.

   Example

   Coming events cast shadow.

Coming – present participle
Events – noun

B) It can work as a complement to the subject; it is used after a link verb or verb of incomplete predication.

Example
> The **film** was **interesting**.
> Interesting – present participle (adjective); modifies the word film.

C) Object complement

Example
> I saw **him swimming** in the river.
> Him – object
> Swimming – complement to the object 'him'.

D) Participle phrase modifies a noun.

Example
> The book **lying on the table** is yours.
> The book – noun
> Lying on the table – participle phrase – modifies the noun 'book'.

E) It helps to join two sentences.

Example
> He took his hat in his hand. He went away.
> Ans. Taking his hat in his hand, he went away.

VERBS

Note — Two sentences have been joined by present participle 'taking'.

F) It indicates and lays emphasis on the action which happened first.

Example
>Michelle has passed Senior Secondary Exam. She wants to join college.
>Ans. Having passed Senior Secondary Exam, Michelle wants to join college.

G) All the ing forms which show continuous tense are present participle.

Example
>They **are working**.
>They **were cooking** lunch.
>My mother **will be going** to Delhi.
>Rahel **has been working** hard all these months.

Formation of present participle

Verb	Present participle
Is, are, am, was, were, be	being
Bend, bent	bending
Run, ran	running
Has, have	having
Pick, picked	picking
Had	having
Tear	tearing

Exercise 1

Identify present participle and find out which noun it modifies or the way it is working.

1) One of us saw **him jumping** out of the window.

   Answer : Pronoun him, jumping present participle, present participle is object complement.

2) Each of us has seen those **winding streets**.

   Answer : Winding present participle, streets verb complement

3) He is driving fast.

4) The man standing in the corner is a police man.

5) We have no running water.

6) Leaving the room untidy, she went off to sleep.

7) Mother left them playing with their toys.

8) The exercise was tiring.

9) Having paid three times, he doesn't want to continue studies.

10) Rahel **has been supporting** the family for a long time.

    Question : In what way are the following words working?

    Has been supporting

    (give the answer)

11) The train arriving now has brown paint.

12) His words left me thinking.

13) Seeing the teacher coming towards them the boys stopped talking.

14) We found the child crying.

15) Talking loudly, Raju tried to disturb the class.

VERBS

Present participles are used after object pronouns

Subject pronoun	Object pronoun
I	me
she	her
he	him
we	us
you	you
It	it

> present participle – ing form of the verb is used after object pronouns and nouns

Exercise 2:

Make complete sentences using suitable nouns or pronouns and present participle to complete the predicates.

Example:

She heard me singing when she entered the room.

1. He saw --
2. You left ---
3. We found --
4. The detective caught ---
5. The farmer saw ---
6. All of us heard --
7. The captain left--
8. I found my sister ---
9. The observer caught the fisherman ---------------------------------
10. They have left the horse ---

Exercise 3 : Jumbled words

Arrange the given words into sentences using one word as present participle.

Example: limped/ moved/wounded/the/aside/man
Answer : limping the wounded man moved aside.
1. there/the/sat/violin/man/play/blind/the
2. bed/i/think/in/lay
3. he/gaze/somebody/spoke to
4. tom/the newspaper/read/breakfast/his/ate
5. lesson/sat/the/class/the/in/inspector/watch/ the
6. ran/the fat/chase/man/bus/the
7. from/begged/the/door/went/door/to/old/man

Exercise 4 :-

Arrange the given words into sentences use the wrong words correctly.
1. an old man, saw, i, cross the road
2. will see, shoot a film, you, some people
3. none of us, him, has heard, sing
4. the mechanic, the clock, work, set
5. the tv, carry on, the operation, the doctor, showed.
6. don't you, something, smell, burn
7. notice, we, the policeman, stand at the gate

Note :

The verbs changed into – ing (present participle) form to join two sentences
1) She is busy. She can't see you now.
   being busy, she can't see you now.
2) She sat in the park. She admired the flowers.
   sitting in the park, she admired the flowers.

3) I cooked dinner. I took bath.

   having cooked the dinner, i took bath.

Exercise 5:-

Join the following sentences using present participle as shown above.

1) It was warm inside the room. We sat outside.
2) She had cooked the dinner. She laid the table.
3) The thief took out the revolver. He threatened her.
4) I have promised him to help. I must not back out.
5) The teacher raised his voice. He told the boys to stop talking.
6) He switched off the light. He went to bed.
7) The price was too high. I didn't buy the car.
8) The prices have gone up. The workers are asking for higher wages.
9) I believed the beggar's story. I gave him money.
10) There was no high school in the village. The boys had to walk 2 miles to the town.
11) He had worked the whole day. He needed rest.
12) The robbers saw the police man. They ran away.
13) We have taken the decision. Let us stick to it.
14) She lost her ring. She began to cry.
15) He did his homework. He went for a walk.
16) I was standing in front of my house. I saw a unique bird.
17) The party was over. The guests dispersed.
18) The sun rose. We went out for a walk.
19) The house was fallen down. Te lives in out house.

20) The match was over. The players sat to rest.
21) The battle was over. The soldiers returned home.
22) I saw a snake coming towards me. I ran away.
23) The mob was shouting slogans. The mob looted the shop.
24) The criminal hid behind the house. The criminal shot at the police.
25) The artist bent the stick. The artist formed different shapes with it.

Past Participle

Past participle has different functions. At times it acts as an adverbial adjective. Past participle is formed by adding ed, en, n or by making internal changes in the simple present(present indeed finite tense) of a verb.

Simple Present Tense   Past Participle

Simple Present Tense	Past Participle
look	looked
talk	talked
laugh	laughed
shake	shaken
blow	blown
throw	thrown
tear	torn
teach	taught
buy	bought

The underlined nouns are modified by past participle

rotten eggs

torn shoes

fractured leg

VERBS

frozen vegetables
uprooted trees
folded sheets
decorated house
soiled shoes
embroidered dress
wounded soldiers

Example. 1

Answer the following questions using the words given above or others

1. What kind of dresses does she like?
2. When certain vegetables are out of season what kind of vegetables can you cook?
3. What kind of shoes do we take to the cobbler?
4. What dirties a house?
5. What needs to be plastered?
6. Who needs blood the most?
7. What do you find inside the envelopes?
8. What is the cause of traffic jam?
9. What did the mother throw out of the vessel?
10. What kind of houses do you see on diwali?

Exercise. 2

Join the following using past participle

Example

The master of the house looked at the plants. The plants were withered

Answer-

The master of the house looked at the withered plants

1. The washerman brought the clothes, the clothes were washed in the stream.
2. The doctor bandaged john's leg. It was twisted.
3. They dug out the goods. The goods were damaged by fire.
4. Father brought the medicines. The medicine was prescribed by the doctor.
5. Mr. smith polished the furniture. The furniture was worn out.
6. I saw the vase. The vase was broken by one of my brothers.
7. The shopkeeper displayed the dress. The dress was embroidered.
8. His parents provided him with best opportunities. His parents were inspired by his performance.
9. He has been cheated once. He is more careful now.
10. The man was wanted by the police. He lay in hiding.
11. He has been invited to speak on college day. He is preparing the speech.
12. The king had been betrayed by the minister. He had to yield to his enemy.
13. The prisoner was charged with murder. He pleaded not guilty.
14. The house was decorated with colorful lights. It looked beautiful.
15. The goods had been damaged. They had to be sold at a lower price.
16. He had been dismissed from his post. He left the city.

+ Perception and − Perception verbs
+ Perception verbs (With different structures)

Since perception plays a dominant role in forming these verbs, they are named as + perception verbs. Eyes, help us to see, nose helps us to smell, ears help us to hear, skin helps us to feel, tongue helps us to taste.

List of Verbs

See, hear, smell, taste, notice, recognize, watch

These words can't be used in continuous form as they indicate state not action.

Example one

She is seeing the flower. (Wrong)

Active voice sentence structure is as follows:

Example two

Active voice sentence structure is as follows :

(a) I **saw him walk** past my window.

   Saw is a + perception verb

   Him is an object

   Walk is an infinitive without to

(b) I **saw him walking** past my window.

   Walking is present participle

Note: Both sentences a & b are right

Passive voice sentence structure form is as follows :

(a) He **was seen to walk** past my window

   Was seen is a + perception verb

   To walk is to + infinitive

(b) He was seen walking past my window

Walking is present participle / ing form

Note:

If the given sentence has infinitive in active voice, the infinitive takes 'to' in the passive voice.

As walk is infinitive in the active voice

To walk is an infinitive in the passive voice.

Present participle (ing form) remains the same both in active and passive voice.

A sentence with the verb 'smell' should always take present participle (ing form) after its object

As

I smell something burning. **right**

I smell something burn. X

I smell something to burn X

The first sentence is right in its active voice.

Passive Voice

Something is smelt burning. **right**

Exercise One :

1.1 Change the following sentences into passive voice.

(a) Some of us have seen him pass by your house.

(b) They heard the thief call out my name.

(c) The guard saw some of you enter the building.

(d) I noticed the boy trip over a stone.

(e) Children will hear you whistling.

(f) We saw the ship leave the dock at four O'clock.

VERBS

(g) Let me see the ship sailing by.

(h) The police recognized the thief climbing up the ladder.

1.2 Complete the following sentences choosing the correct alternative.

(a) I saw your father _____ (talking, to talk) with someone.

(b) As soon as they heard you _____ (whistle, to whistle), they came out of their houses.

(c) Food was smelt _____ (burn, to burn, burning).

(d) The teacher noticed my class mate _____ (to peep, peep) out of the window.

(e) My class mate was noticed _____ (cheat, to cheat) from another student's paper.

(f) She recognized me _____ (to wear, wearing) my red dress.

(g) Let us hear the bell _____ (to ring, ringing).

(h) The team was seen _____ (leave, to leave) the stadium.

-Perception Verbs

These are –perception verbs because organs of perception like eyes, ears, nose, tongue do not play a major roll.

Group One

Make, let, have, bit, help

Sentence structures for the verb 'make'.

Active voice :-   Mother made the child finish his meal.
'Made' is a verb
'The child' is an object,
'Finish' is an infinitive without 'to'.

Passive voice :-   The child was made to finish his meal.
'Was made' is a verb
'To finish' is an infinitive with 'to'.

Structures of the verb 'let'.

Active voice :-   She lets me repeat the answer again and again.
'Lets' is a verb
'Me' is an object
'Repeat' is an infinitive without 'to'.

Note : A sentence with 'let' can't change into passive voice.

Structure of the verb 'have'.

Active voice :   The police had him reveal the truth.
'Had' is a verb
'Him' is an object
'Reveal' is an infinitive without 'to'.

Note : A sentence with 'had' can't be changed into passive voice.

Structures of the verb 'bid'.

Active voice :   The director bade him leave.
'Bade' is a verb
'Him' is an object
'Leave' is an infinitive without 'to'.

Note : 'Bid' isn't used in passive voice; moreover, the verb isn't used in modern English.

Structures of the verb 'Help'.

Active voice : That boy helped me lift the bag.
"helped' is a verb
'Me' is an object
'Lift' is an infinitive without to.
That boy helped me to lift the bag.
(Another form of active voice)
'Helped' is a verb
'Me' is an object
to lift is an infinitive with 'to'.

Passive voice : I was helped to lift the bag.
'was helped' is the verb
'To lift' is an infinitive with 'to'.

Note : The verb help in passive voice is always followed by to + infinitive.

Exercise

1.3 Fill in the blanks with correct form of the given verbs.

(a) The new teacher made him _____ hard. (work, to work)

(b) Our neighbor helped us _____ fruit. (gathering, gathered, gather)

(c) I was made _____ at the gate until the chief guest arrived. (to wait, wait, waiting)

(d) The head cook should be helped _____ the dinner prepared. (get, got, to get)

(e) Will you let him _____? (Study, to study, studying)

(f) When will she be made _____ for the interview? (to appear, appear, appearing)

(g) Make the horse _____ out a little faster. (step, to step, stepping)

(h) Are students being helped _____ the party? (arrange, to arrange)

Group B -Perception Verbs
List of verbs
Leave, catch, find, get, start, keep

Sentences with the given verb take the given structure

Verb + Object + ing from of the verb (active voice)

Verb + ing form of the verb (passive voice)

Example

Active voice : Mother caught Rita tearing the dress.
'Caught' is a verb
'Rita' is an object
'Tearing' is –ing form

Passive voice : Rita was caught tearing the dress.
'Was' caught is a verb
'tearing' –ing form

Note : If 'to' +infinitive is used instead of ing form, the meaning of the sentence changes completely or the sentence looks senseless.

As – Mother caught Rita to tear the dress. X (senseless)

Rita was caught to tear the dress. X

Exercise

1.4 Re-write the following sentences

Example : when I caught him, he was eating jam.

VERBS

Answer : I caught him eating jam.

(a) When one of the students found her, she was copying notes.

(b) The boy was threshing grain when the farmer left him.

(c) When the left, the child was sleeping.

(d) When the police caught the thief, he was breaking the safe.

1.5 Complete the given sentences

(a) The driver kept the engine _____ for quite sometime. (run, to run, running)

(b) Get the car _____; otherwise its engine will cease. (moving, move, to move)

(c) The teacher left the class _____ notes. (Copy, to copy, copying)

(d) The principal caught Tom _____ over the wall. (jumping, to jump, jump)

(e) Our neighbours found the stranger _____ information. (collect, to collect, collecting)

(f) The discussion was kept _____ in spite of heated arguments. (going, go, to go)

Note : your answer shouldn't show purpose.

1.6 Change the following sentences into passive voice

(a) As I hadn't completed my homework, the teacher made me stay back to complete my home task.

(b) While Ramu was ploughing the field, Chandran helped mother.

(c) I can make him understand the situation.

(d) We saw some children plucking flowers.

(e) Rani has heard him pronounce this word correctly.
(f) Sometimes I hear the birds chirping.
(g) The doctor will make you take these injections.
(h) Have you seen that beggar roaming on this road.
(i) If you want, she can help you.
(j) She always makes me clean the table.
(k) You ought to see Meena dancing.
(l) Please make Rahul work hard; otherwise he will fail.
(m) Because she has heard you abusing them, she can't respect you anymore.
(n) The child couldn't sleep as he heard the dog barking.
(o) The principal will make the students obey school regulations.

1.7 Change the following sentences into active voice.

(a) My father is made to take his medicines regularly by my mother.
(b) He was heard to spell out the words.
(c) Have I been heard talking loudly by anyone?
(d) Has he ever been helped by his friend?
(e) Will I be made to deliver this letter?
(f) She has been seen shopping by one of her neighbours.
(g) Can I be helped to carry this bag?
(h) I am made to clean the house many times.

Answers
Exercise 1.1

(a) He has been seen to pass by your house.
(b) The thief was heard to call out my name.
(c) Some of you were seen to enter the building.

VERBS

(d) The boy was noticed to trip over a stone.
(e) You will be heard whistling by the children.
(f) The ship was seen to leave the dock at 4' o'clock.
(g) Let the ship be seen sailing by.
(h) The thief was recognized climbing up the ladder.

Exercise 1.2

(a) Talking
(b) Whistle
(c) Burning
(d) Peep
(e) To cheat
(f) Wearing
(g) Ringing
(h) To leave

Exercise 1.3

(a) Work
(b) Gather
(c) To wait
(d) To get
(e) To study
(f) To appear
(g) Step
(h) To arrange

Exercise 1.4

(a) One of the students found her copying notes.
(b) The farmer left the boy threshing grain.

(c) They left the child sleeping.
(d) The police caught the thief breaking the safe.

Exercise 1.5

(a) Running
(b) Moving
(c) Copying
(d) Jumping
(e) Collecting
(f) Going

Exercise 1.6

(a) As I hadn't completed my homework, I was made to stay back and complete it.
(b) While Ramu was plowing the field, mother was helped by Chanderan.
(c) He can be made to understand the situation by.
(d) Some children were seen plucking flowers.
(e) He has been heard to pronounce this word correctly by Rani.
(f) Sometimes the birds are heard chirping.
(g) You will be made to take these injections by the doctor.
(h) Has the beggar been seen roaming on this road?
(i) If you want, you can be helped by her.
(j) I am always made to clean the table.
(k) Meena ought to be seen dancing.
(l) Let Rahul be made to work hard; otherwise, he will fail.
(m) Because you have been heard abusing them, she can't respect you anymore.

VERBS

(n) The child couldn't sleep as the dog was heard barking.

(o) The students will be made to obey school regulations.

Exercise 1.7

(a) My mother makes my father take his medicines regularly.

(b) Someone heard him spell out the words.

(c) Has anyone heard me talking loudly?

(d) Has his friend ever helped him?

(e) Will make me deliver this letter?

(f) One of our neighbours has seen her shopping.

(g) Can you help me carry this bag?

(h) They make me clean the house many times.

Verb Agreement
Section A
Rules :

1. Two or more singular subjects connected by 'and' usually take a plural verb.
2. If singular nouns refer to the same person or thing, the verb must be singular.
3. If two subjects together express one idea, the verb can be singular.
4. If the singular subjects are preceded by 'each' or 'every', the verb is usually singular.
5. Two or more singular subjects connected by or, either or, neither --- nor take a verb in singular form.

Note : The subject should agree with its verb. This problem occurs mostly with simple present, present continuous and present perfect tense….. do, does, has, have, is, are, was, were. Since the past tense doesn't take an 's', this problem doesn't occur. Functional verbs in simple present tense take 's' if the subject is singular as : Raju plays football. If the subject is plural, the verb doesn't take an 's' as : Girls like dolls.

- According to the rules given above choose the correct alternative from the clues. Fill in the blanks in simple present, present continuous or present perfect tense

A

1. Ritu and Neetu _____ (be) good friends.
2. Fire and water _____ (not agree).
3. Anjali, Kamal and Ramesh _____ (not go) to the same school.
4. He and his friend _____ (been working hard all these months.
5. Roses _____ (has, have) different colours.

B

1. My friend and benefactor _____ (present perfect). Verb 'be'
2. The orator and statesman _____ (be, simple present) out of town.
3. The captain and adjutant _____ (work, present perfect continuous tense) over these files.
4. By the death of Mahatma Gandhi, a great statesman and patriot _____ (be, simple past) a great loss to India.

C

1. Bread and milk _____ (be, simple present) his only food.
2. The horse and carriage _____ (be) at the door.
3. The long and the short of the matter _____ (be) this.

VERBS

4. Slow and steady _____ (win) the race.
5. Early to bed and early to rise _____ (make) man healthy wealthy and wise.

D

1. Every boy and girl _____ (train) by the instructor.
2. Every man and woman in the village _____ (praise, present continuous) him for his literacy campaign)
3. No nook or corner _____ (be, simple past) left unexplored.
4. Neither he nor I _____ (be, simple past) there.
5. Neither Meera nor her sister _____ (awarded, present perfect).
6. Neither food nor water _____ (take) by him for three days.
7. Neither praise nor blame _____ (seem) to affect him.

Rules :

1. When the subject is joined by or, nor, are different numbers, the verb must be plural and the plural subject must be placed before verb.
2. When the subjects joined by 'or', 'nor' are of different persons, the verb agrees in person with the verb nearest to it.
3. A collective noun takes a singular verb when the collection is thought of as a whole. A plural verb is used when the individuals of the whole are indicated separately.

E
Fill in the blanks in different forms of present tense

1. Ali or his brother _____ (dig) present perfect this well.
2. Neither the headmaster nor his assistants _____ (arrive, present perfect)

3. Neither the mother nor her daughters _____ (be simple present) injured.
4. Either the boy or his parents _____ (make, present perfect) this mistake.

F

1. Either he or I _____ (be, mistake)
2. Neither you nor he _____ (to be blame)
3. Either the meat on the tray or the fish in the plate _____ (be) stale.
4. Neither my children nor yours _____ (call, present perfect) by the head mistress.
5. Either the cat or the puppies _____ (tear, present perfect) my book.
6. Neither my money nor yours _____ (deposit, present perfect) in our accounts.

G

1. The Council _____ (choose, present perfect) its president.
2. The fleet _____ (set, present perfect) sail.
3. The committee _____ (decide, present perfect) what stand it should take.
4. The committee _____ (be, divided)
5. The majority of the people _____ (appear, appears) to be against the decision.
6. The crew _____ (know/knows) their duties.
7. At first the jury _____ (be, simple past divide) in their opinion but finally it _____ (return, present perfect) to its unanimous verdict.

VERBS

Fill in the blanks using is, are, am, was, were, have, has

1. The teacher as well as students _____ absent.
2. There _____ many objections to this plan.
3. Neither his father nor his mother _____ alive.
4. It _____ difficult to get pure butter and milk.
5. Iron as well as coper _____ scarce in that country.
6. The committee _____ going to choose its president.
7. The public _____ (request) not to walk on the grass.
8. The notorious dacoit with his followers _____ (been capture)
9. Forty yards _____ a good distance.
10. The great poet and novelist _____ (die)
11. None of you _____ (done) his work properly.
12. Each of the boys _____ (awarded).
13. The accountant and the cashier _____ (been caught) note 'the indicates two separate people.
14. The Chief with his followers _____ (is, are) in his office.

   Note : The nouns which are placed before 'with', along with, as well as, together with will agree with the verb.

15. No news _____ (be) good news.
16. Extravagance as well as parsimony _____ (to be avoid)
17. A good man and useful citizen _____ (has, have, pass) away.
18. Man's happiness or misery _____ (be) in his own hands.
19. Kindness as well as justice _____ (should go hand in hand)

20. Gulliver's Travels _____ (be) written by swift.
21. The strain of all the difficulties, vexation anxieties _____ (be) more than he could bear.
22. One or the other of those fellows _____ (steal, present perfect) the watch.
23. Each of the suspected men _____ (arrest)
24. The formation of paragraphs _____ (build) up the plot.
25. That night every one of the crew _____ (be) down with fever.
26. Cows as well as horses _____ (eat) grass.
27. Two third of the city _____ (be) ruined.
28. Which one of these umbrellas _____ (be) yours.
29. One of the arguments he offered _____ (seems) convincing.
30. The administration of various interests and districts so remote _____ (demand) / demands) no common capacity and vigour.

Editing

Section 1 : Edit the following sentences. Write the wrong word and next to it its correct word. Follow the same instructions

A

I told him that I will visit that place
the following year. He replied that there is
no hurry you could make it later
on. I asked him why he is so concerned

a. _____ _____
b. _____ _____
c. _____ _____
d. _____ _____

VERBS

about mine timings. Some
how our   e. _____ _____
discussion ends and we   f. _____ _____
leave the place. On our way
we met   g. _____ _____
some friends of our and   h. _____ _____
have a pleasant talk   i. _____ _____

B

Edit - Correct the wrong word.

The thiefs didn't open the   a. _____ _____
door.
and jumped over the fence   b. _____ _____
one of them fall down   c. _____ _____
and couldn't help scream.   d. _____ _____
His shin bone have   e. _____ _____
broken.
It was dangling as if   f. _____ _____
something was tie with a   g. _____ _____
rope.
His companions got   h. _____ _____
panick
and did not knew what to   i. _____ _____
do

C

Edit - correct the wrong word.

Instead of go ahead with   a. _____ _____
their mission, the thief had   b. _____ _____
to take care of their liable.   c. _____ _____
They were in the   d. _____ _____
dangerous

59

of be caught. While the   e. _____ _____
injure man was taken care   f. _____ _____
of
flash lights bright the   g. _____ _____
scene.
The police run to the scene   h. _____ _____
but arrested the criminals   i. _____ _____

D

Edit - Correct the wrong word.

There was deadly silent   a. _____ _____
all over the
town. Spell of sleep had   b. _____ _____
bring things
to stand still. It was   c. _____ _____
2 a.m. and a
mother is tending to her   d. _____ _____
sick baby.
Suddenly she hear   e. _____ _____
rumbling and tumbling
around her. She rock in   f. _____ _____
her bed
along with her baby. The   g. _____ _____
walls start
swinging. The roof fall   h. _____ _____
down

E

Edit - correct the wrong word.

Both the baby and the   a. _____ _____
mother were horrible
stricken. The mother lays   b. _____ _____
over the baby.

VERBS

Just than a be am landed on the mother.	c. _____ _____
she groan for a moment and then	d. _____ _____
become cold. Her baby was left in God's care.	e. _____ _____
There was darkness and the baby cling to its	f. _____ _____
mother's breast squeal as if it was	g. _____ _____
Tease by the fairies around.	h. _____ _____

Section 2 :

Edit, write the wrong word correctly.

F

Learning is a life-long processes.	a. _____ _____
Man learns until his death day.	b. _____ _____
Learning take place not	c. _____ _____
around in the classroom	d. _____ _____
but also in day to day live.	e. _____ _____
A two year child stay	f. _____ _____
on home but keeps busy.	g. _____ _____
When he was awake, what	h. _____ _____
do he do?	i. _____ _____
Don't it look like a nuisance?	j. _____ _____

G

When he tears a peace of paper,   a. _____

and throw the bits all around   b. _____

the house, he actions like a   c. _____

doctor and thirsts a needle   d. _____

onto the hand of a doll.   e. _____

H

A girl child pretence to be a mother   a. _____

and play house   b. _____

with hers playmates.   c. _____

Before going to school, Children   d. _____

starts playing with block.   e. _____

Mothers try to made them   f. _____

recognize different colours.

Section 3 :

Edit – correct the wrong words

I

I told my friend your bag was   a. _____

heavy than   b. _____

my. I can comfortably   c. _____

lift my bag and wander.   d. _____

How do she manage to carry   e. _____

her. During rainy season   f. _____

when I doesn't carry my   g. _____

VERBS

umbrella, my clothe and
bag get wet and became
heavy than before.
My shoes get filled
on water and makes
squeaking sound

h. _____ _____
i. _____ _____
j. _____ _____
k. _____ _____
l. _____ _____
m. _____ _____

J

Does we look funny
when we get complete drenched
on muddy rain water?
Once at such a rainy day,
I was offer a lift by my friend.
I told her I can manage without a lift
because my house is nearby, however
I don't want to spil her new car
Dew to my dirty, muddy clothes.

a. _____ _____
b. _____ _____
c. _____ _____
d. _____ _____
e. _____ _____
f. _____ _____
g. _____ _____
h. _____ _____
i. _____ _____

Section 4 :

Error : Edit – correct the wrong words

K

The victims of an earthquake suffer a lot. They are render homeless;

a. _____ _____
b. _____ _____

their houses turn into moands of rubble   c. _____

under which dead bodys and   d. _____

injury people groan, moan and sigh.   e. _____

Suddenly there is a dead clam.   f. _____

Chilly winds sent shivers. A few   g. _____

People stand near the heeps with   h. _____

a stare look. It is a   i. _____

Hart rending site. Oh God!   j. _____

We are your create. We pray   k. _____

Thee to be mercy to us   l. _____

L

Your friend had been waiting from   a. _____

you since four hours. As you   b. _____

did not turned up, he decided   c. _____

to went and attend a meeting.   d. _____

He leave this message for you as   e. _____

he had some urgent matter to attend   f. _____

Section 5 :

Error : Edit – write the wrong word correctly

M

I has been improving my English	a.	_____ _____
since I come to this school.	b.	_____ _____
There have been many changes about me.	c.	_____ _____
I like to give time to this	d.	_____ _____
subject and tries to speak	e.	_____ _____
in English. My English teacher teach	f.	_____ _____
us with dedication and pleasant.	g.	_____ _____
The whole class love to attend her classes	h.	_____ _____

N

Polar regions are covered on snow.	a.	_____ _____
Eatables are scare. It is difficult	b.	_____ _____
to makes two ends meet. Fish	c.	_____ _____
and meat are their daily diet.	d.	_____ _____
Snow destroy what they	e.	_____ _____
grows. Ever green trees are	f.	_____ _____

mostly covered with   g. _____
snow. People
cover themselves with   h. _____
fur which they get from i. _____
their hunt
animals. Their food is   j. _____
cook
with the fat which they k. _____
get from
blubber who comes from   l. _____
whales
and other sea animals.   m. _____
Thanks to
modern technology which n. _____
is try to make
their live better.   f. _____

Omitting

One word is missing in each line, write it between two words it is missing.

A

The monkey was sitting on a roof   a. Monkey **which** was sitting

eating ripe bananas, saw   b. _____

some children. He started making   c. _____

faces. Children started teasing him.   d. _____

The monkey furious and climbed up a tree.   e. _____

He started to throw sticks them.   f. _____

VERBS

One of the children hit on his head. Children got scared ran away.	g. _____ h. _____ i. _____

B

My husband and I chose beautiful	a. _____
Carved sofa set. It was very	b. _____
Expensive. It was Rupees fifteen thousand.	c. _____
We looked it in other shops.	d. _____
After going shop to shop, we	e. _____
eyed one was very much the same	f. _____
the one we liked before. Fortunately,	g. _____
it was Rupees five thousand less.	h. _____
Immediately decided to buy it.	i. _____
We made payments and got it loaded.	j. _____
It was best shopping we ever did.	k. _____

C

It is not good claim that one's	a. _____
job is most important than that of	b. _____
others. Each profession needs dedication.	c. _____

Our services should done dutifully and conscientiously. Then only one expect desired results.

d. _____
e. _____
f. _____

D

Do you know how this dish cooked? All your customers myself relish this food. I want to cook this dish other special occasions. Since I am hotel industry, I feel it is better serve a variety of delicious dishes so that our customers attracted go home satisfied pleasant similes on their faces..

a. _____
b. _____
c. _____
d. _____
e. _____
f. _____
g. _____
h. _____
i. _____
j. _____

E

Mother puts the lights before she goes sleep. She makes it sure that doors windows are properly locked. Sometimes I help her closing

a. _____
b. _____
c. _____
d. _____

VERBS

the house. We, the younger are not   e. _____ _____ _____

careful as she is. Sooner later we   f. _____ _____ _____

have to become serious concerning   g. _____ _____ _____

our security well as of others.   h. _____ _____ _____

F

Karim treated Gajpati gentleness   a. _____ _____ _____

because trusted him.   b. _____ _____ _____

Karim's wife used fetch water   c. _____ _____ _____

the Tapti River. In the absence of Karim   d. _____ _____ _____

and his wife, Gajpati took care   e. _____ _____ _____

their child. They used put the child   f. _____ _____ _____

the middle   g. _____ _____ _____

a chircle and tied Gajpati's foot   h. _____ _____ _____

chains to a tree.   i. _____ _____ _____

Gajpati took care the child.   j. _____ _____ _____

Once when the parents to town,   k. _____ _____ _____

Gajpati had tough time. One night   l. _____ _____ _____

when hyenas to attack the child.   m. _____ _____ _____

The baby restless and tried to   n. ___ ___ ___
get of the circle. One of the hyenas   o. ___ ___ ___
came quite close to baby; Gajpati   p. ___ ___ ___
stood quietly and crushed   q. ___ ___ ___
the hyena to pulp. Gajpati   r. ___ ___ ___
curled baby in his trunk   s. ___ ___ ___
and kept it of danger. Gajpati   t. ___ ___ ___
seriously injured but looked   u. ___ ___ ___
peaceful as did his duty   v. ___ ___ ___
and didn't care himself.   w. ___ ___ ___
Uprooting tree caused him serious   x. ___ ___ ___
Injuries.   ___ ___ ___

G

One of my friends who comes   a. ___ ___ ___
my neighbourhood told me her   b. ___ ___ ___
miraculous escape. Three days ago she   c. ___ ___ ___
taking her little sister to school which d. ___ ___ ___
is close to house.   e. ___ ___ ___
There is a dense cluster trees nearby. f. ___ ___ ___

VERBS

When she passed it, she heard some sounds	g. _____ _____ _____
It sent shivers her body and she started to	h. _____ _____ _____
tremble. Her legs had strength. After a while	i. _____ _____ _____
She gained control herself and looked back.	j. _____ _____ _____
She saw robbers collecting booty. I told my	k. _____ _____ _____
Sister to go school. The robbers were wearing	l. _____ _____ _____
masks and their pistols.	m. _____ _____ _____
The road was lonely I kept running.	n. _____ _____ _____
Suddenly police man saved me.	o. _____ _____ _____

Jumbled Words

Jumbled words to be arranged into sentences

Note : Different types of adjective should be placed in their correct order before a subject noun or the noun in the predicate part of a sentence.

A

Only five brave volunteers are needed

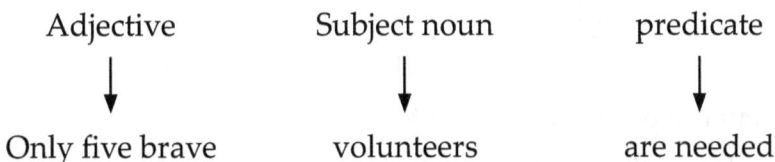

Adjective	Subject noun	predicate
↓	↓	↓
Only five brave	volunteers	are needed

B

Subject   The traveler needs fresh, delicious, vegetarian lunch

↓

The traveler   adjective

Needs fresh, delicious vegetarian noun lunch

Predicate

A

Arrange the following words into sentences

1. Monuments / by / tourists / gilded / are / the / magnificent / visited / are
2. Specially / only / their / of / six / awarded / were / animals / fattened
3. All / nearly / of / intelligent / students / my / jobs / selected / been / have / for / those
4. Lively / her / is / child / pleasant / and / going / take / the / competition / in / to / part
5. Cut / these / well / new / knives
6. Completed / been / has / task / difficult / almost / this / of / half
7. Story / quite / was / the / horrible
8. Children / only / few / like / a / games / indoor

B

Nouns in the predicate of a sentence

1. Like / if / you / away / give / of / some / books / your
2. Took / student / of / some / books / my / important / a

VERBS

3. Me / that / my / he / friend / interesting / told / written / has / three / very / novels
4. One / across / came / I / yesterday / friends / of / old / my
5. Has / tricky / solve / Ravi / been / to / able / almost / your / of / riddles / all / complicated
6. Steep / neither / climb / the / climbers / could / of / climbs / up those
7. a / people / few / the / only / take / guide / will / time / a / at
8. Exciting / show / magician / the / us / tricks / three / will

Arranging Jumbled Words into complete Sentences

A

Make sentences using the jumbled words

1. Man / practice / perfect / makes / and / gains / efforts / through / perfection / continuous
2. Flowers beds / dug / the / themselves / they / grew / and / flowers
3. Confidence / have / that / I / will / interview / pass / this / he
4. He / into / threw / garbage / dustbin / the
5. Their / not / ball / this / is
6. Sweets / didn't / which / she / the / take / offered / her / to /I
7. Themselves / girls / have / those / made / dresses / these
8. Truth / your / there / in / statement / is
9. In / the / trinkets / woman / her / beautiful / has / hair
10. Difficult / drive / it / to / rough / on / is / road / this
11. Ponds / do / in / area / this / around / the / you / fish / find
12. This / a / of / has / forest / destroyed / herd / elephants / by / been

13. Friendship / when / she / false / against / accusation / me / broke / made / our
14. We / there / a / hotel / in / room / book / as / reach / soon / as / we / will / a

B

1. Pollution / believe / that / they / day / is / by / day / increasing
2. Since / living / they / in / have / Gurugram / been / 1990
3. If / been / had / you / given / an / such / opportunity / would / it / accepted / have / you
4. Stormy / it / such / evening / is / a / chief / that / may / the executive / delayed / be
5. Was / into / pan / baking / a / batter / the / poured / then / and / it /baked / was
6. Is / to / aids / incurable /considered / be
7. To / Rohit / Principal / the / allow / requested / him / tell / to / problem / his / him / to
8. The / ordered / leave / captain / crew / positions / they / to / the / not / until / to / told / their / they / do / so / they / were

Present Participle and Perfect Participle (used to make subordinate clauses)

Introduction :

1. Change simple past tense in –ing form or having + past participle whichever is appropriate.
2. Use subordinate clauses

VERBS

Join the following sentences using the given clues
A.

Example : Clues are in brackets

1. We were tired of the journey. We sat under a tree. (because and present participle)

   Answer : Because we were tired of the journey, we sat under a tree.

2. Being tired of the journey, we sat under a tree.
3. She lost her ring. She began to cry. (as, having)
4. He completed his paper. He gave it to the teacher. (after, having)
5. Rahul took a bath. Rahul went to school. (having)
6. He did his home-task. He played some music. (having)
7. The captain raised his gun. The captain aimed at the enemy. (raising)
8. I walked towards the field. I saw a snake.(-ing)
9. Nirmal was standing in front of his house. Nirmal saw some naughty children throwing stones at a dog. (-ing)
10. I sat with my friends. I drew some sketches. (-ing)
11. The mob created havoc. The mob shouted slogans. (-ing)
12. The players played brilliantly. They were awarded. (-ing or having)

B. Using absolute phrase, join the following sentences. When subjects of two sentences are different, the sentences are joined using absolute phrases (subjects of both the sentences are used)

1. The Sun rose. We went out for a walk.

   Answer:

   (A) The Sun having risen, we went out for a walk. - ing can also be used.

   (B) As the sun rose, we went out for a walk. (Reason clause)

2. It is very hot. We can not continue our journey.
3. His house has fallen down. He lives in the out house.
4. The weather was fine. We went on a picnic.
5. Mother got worried for my younger brother. We set out in his search.
6. The bell rang. The boys went out of their classrooms.
7. The match was over. The players sat down to rest.
8. The battle was over. The soliders entered the town.
9. The dinner was delicious. The guests praised it.
10. The ship sank. The crew were drowned.
11. The patient was restless. The doctor couldn't sleep the whole night.
12. The dog was itchy. The doctor was consulted.

C. Using to + infinitive join the given sentences.

1. I want to go to the city. I have to buy good furniture.

   Answer: I want to go to the city to buy good furniture.

2. He has two sons. He must educate them.
3. Raj is very weak. He can not walk
4. My father was pleased. He heard of my success.
5. Renu is going to Mumbai. She wants to visit her parents.

D. Join the given sentences using a preposition followed by a noun or a gerund.

VERBS

Prepositions : without, on, by, with, in spite of, despite, after.
Change the underlined words into ing form or noun form.

1. He heard of his success. He was very happy.

    Answer : On hearing of his success he was very happy.

2. He wrote the complaint. He **hesitated**.
3. He wrote the complaint. He didn't **hesitate**.
4. He is **poor**. He is honest.
5. His mother **died**. He heard the news. He felt grieved.
6. He could not go to school. He was **ill**.
7. I **helped** my friend, otherwise he would have been ruined.
8. He was **defeated**. He was disappointed.
9. A kind hearted man saved the child. He **risked** his life.
10. The good Samaritan **saw** an injured man on the road. He bandaged the poor man's wounds. He took him to a good hospital and paid for his medication.

E. Join the following sentences using a phrase in apposition.

1. Sohan was an intelligent man. He had control over his temper.

    Answer : Sohan, an intelligent man had control over his temper. ('an intelligent man' is in apposition.

2. Delhi is the capital of India. Political meetings are held here.
3. Shakespeare was a great literary figure. He wrote many dramas and poems.
4. Tagore was a great Indian poet. He won international fame.
5. Edison invented the gramophone. Edison was a great inventor.

6. Hiroshima was once a prosperous town. It still bears the after effects of the past bomb.
7. Wordsworth was born in 1770. He was a great English poet.
8. Tsunami is an extremely destructive force. Tsunami sweeps away all that comes on its way.

F. Join the given sentences using an adverb or an adverbial phrase. Note : Adverbs will take-ly some adverbs can be placed first.

1. He is honest. His honesty is **perfect**.

   Answer : He is perfectly honest.
2. The pedestrian was wounded. His wound was **fatal**.
3. That girl failed in the examination. It was **unfortunate**.
4. The Sun set. The trees appeared **dim**.
5. He will rank first. This is **certain**.
6. He was absent from school. His absence was **intentional**.
7. She refused to help her friend. Her refusal was **firm**.
8. He reached the play ground. He was **punctual**.
9. The chief gave orders to the soliders. The chief was **strict** to give order to the soldiers to move.
10. The maid collected the dirty utensils. She was **reluctant**.

Relative Pronouns and Present Participles

Relative clauses and present participle phrases work like post determiners as they define the noun which comes before it so they work like adjective.

Exercise :

Join the following sentences using relative pronoun and then change the relative clause into present participle phrase.

Examples : the child is my son. He is painting the picture.
Answer :
(a) The child who is painting the picture is my son.
(b) The child painting the picture is my son.

1. The man is my father. He is teaching the class.
2. The Prime Minister met a crowd. The crowd was shouting in the street.
3. The manager lives next door to us. He is dictating letters.
4. The solider fought bravely. He is crossing the road.
5. They caught the prisoner. The prisoner was escaping from the prison.
6. I talked to the child. He was crying in the corner.
7. The merchant is honest. He is selling suitcases.
8. They looked at the flag. The flag was waving in the breeze.
9. They took out a stick. The stick was floating down the stream.
10. The man is our neighbor. He is ploughing the field.
11. They photographed an archaeologist. He was digging out some remnants of pots.
12. Mr. Das noticed a flame. The flame was burning blue in the sky.
13. The Oculist saw a worm in his patients eye. The worm was moving.
14. I was afraid of the ferocious dog. It was barking the whole night.
15. Reena saw her friend. She was passing by her house.

Exercise :

Note the place of the adjectives.

Join the following sentences according to the example.

Example :

She showed me the dress. The dress was torn.

(a) She showed me the dress which was torn.

(b) She showed me the torn dress.

1. He brought the clothes. The clothes were washed in a stream.
2. They were pointing at the temple. The temple wall was painted.
3. The doctor plastered Anil's leg. Anils' leg was twisted.
4. The rescures dug out the dead bodies. The bodies were under the wreckage.
5. The patient took the medicine. The medicine was prescribed.
6. The customer bought the cloth. The cloth was embroidered in traditional style.
7. They carried the box. The box was decorated.
8. They polished the furniture. The furniture was discarded long ago.
9. She showed me her dress. The dress was worn by her friend on a special function.
10. We couldn't get back the vase. The vase was broken by my three year old brother.

Exercise :

Join the following sentences using relative clauses and shortening the second sentence by using to + infinitive

Example :

The film is rated the best. We should see it.

VERBS

Answer :

(a) The film which is rated the best we should be see.

(b) The film rated the best is to be seen.

1. The road goes straight. The road you should take.
2. This is the move. I should practice.
3. This is the dish. You must take it.
4. This is the piece of work. They must do it.
5. This is the essay. I must read.
6. This is the article. We ought to read.
7. This is the officer. He should lead us.
8. This is the boy. He ought to win the match.
9. This is the form. She should fill in.
10. This is the permit. We must take.

Shorten the following sentences according to the example.

Example :

I saw the children who were in the cinema hall.

Answer :

I saw the children in the cinema hall.

Exercise :

1. The boats that were in the harbor have sunk.
2. The buildings which are outside the school have been demolished.
3. The dog which was running on the road has been run over by a car.
4. The cheese which was in the cupboard has been eaten away by rats.

5. The girl who sitting near the window has thrown something.
6. They are repairing the tap which is behind the wall.
7. The girl who is sitting under the tree is my classmate.
8. You must talk to the man who is standing by the gate.
9. The dust which is under the carpet has to be cleaned.
10. They were talking about the car which was in the garage.
11. The book which was on top of the piano has fallen down.
12. The prisoners who in the prison know the details.

Exercise :

Join the following sentences using relative clauses and participle phrases.

1. The spectators nearest the football field started the applause. It was taken up quickly by others in the large crowd.
2. The boy's room was full of his prized possessions. They were tidily arranged on shelves and tables.
3. The thieves were taken completely by surprise. They at first made no attempt to getaway.
4. Raman had a spare seat in the car at the weekend. He at once offered it to his friend, Alok.
5. Manchester is an important Industrial city in Britain. It is frequently visited by businessmen from all over the world.
6. The boy ran back and telephoned for the fire brigade. His house was quite near ours. The fire brigade arrived within a few minutes.
7. They couldn't drive the car into the camping ground. A low wall ran around the entire field. The wall was broken only by a single narrow gateway.

VERBS

8. At one end of the road a tent stood with a table. On the table were piled silver cups and prizes. These had been won during the show.

9. From our house we often saw old Mathews. Old Mathews was Mr. Sing's guard. Old Mathews plodded along the street to the local bar. He often went to the bar for a gossip and a glass of beer.

10. They decided to camp in a field at a bend in the river. They had seen some fishermen there the previous evening. The fishermen were obviously enjoying a good catch.

11. Raju carefully led the injured horse. He went slowly back to the stables. The animal was given the necessary treatment there.

12. The two boys saw an empty hut. They decided to stay the night in it. The boys were walking to Mumbai.

13. Not long afterwards Mr. Misra arrived. He lived very close to our house. He brought us food and warm clothing.

TENSES

Three families of Tenses

A. 1. Present indefinite or simple present
   2. Present Continuous
   3. Preset Perfect
   4. Present Perfect Continuous

B. 1. Past Indefinite or simple Past
   2. Past Continuous
   3. Past Perfect
   4. Past Perfect Continuous

C. 1. Future Indefinite
   2. Future Continuous
   3. Future Perfect
   4. Future Perfect continuous

Tense is the verb form which shows time present past or future. Each tense has its extended functions.

A. Present Indefinite or Simple present; its family

1. Simple Present

1.1 Shows time (present) Ramu **is** here.

1.2 Shows repeated action. A farmer **always** takes care of his crop.

1.3 Shows a fact. Mango **is** a summer fruit.

1.4 Shows truth which is permanent. The sun **gives** light and heat.

2 Present Continuous

2.1 Present Continuous of an action in present time. Examples

We are giving a party today.

But the president is meeting his party tomorrow future plan.

Be verbs – is, are, am (present tense) was, were (past tense continuous 'ing' form is used with 'be' verbs.

Example : is teaching, am teaching, are teaching

Past was reading, was teaching, were teaching.

Note : use 'S' with singular noun in simple present tense.

Example : A student writes a lot. Don't use 'S' with plural noun. Students write a lot. Use 'are' or 'were' with plural nouns or pronoun.

Example :

They are discussing a serious matter. Children are playing now.

Fill up the blanks using present indefinite (Simple Present Tense).

Example :

1. He knows that brave man. (know, knows)
2. The gardener uproots weeds (uproot, uproots)
3. The sun rises in the east. (rise, rises)
4. She is always late. (is, are)
5. Children like to play in the ground. (like, likes)

Sentence : 1. is a fact. 2. Fact. 3. Permanent truth 4. Frequency repeatedly 4. Fact.

Negative form
Example :

1. He does not know that brave man.
2. The gardener does not uproot weeds.
3. The Sun does not rise in the west.
4. She isn't always late
5. Children don't like to play in the ground.

Interrogative form

1. Does he know that brave man?
2. Does the gardener uproot weeds?
3. Does the sun rise in the East?
4. Is she always late?
5. Do the children like to play?

Note : If the verbs has or have, is, are, am, was, were are used alone use them in the given form.

Tom has a new bat

Negative : Tom hasn't a new bat.

Interrogative :

1. a. Has Tom a new bat?
   b. Does Tom have a new bat?
2. They have interesting story books.
   a. Have they interesting story books?
   b. Do they have interesting story books?

TENSES

Note : The usage of 'be' verbs is, are, am, was, were

The students are in the class.

Interrogative : Are the students in the class?

Negative : The students are not in the class.

Don't use do or does when, the verb is, are, am, was, were are used as single verbs.

Practice exercises according to the examples given :

A. Exercise use simple present tense (only simple present tense)

Fill up the blanks. Use the correct choice and then change the sentence into interrogative form and negative form.

1. My friend _____ (work, works)in a town.
2. They _____ (goes, go) to school by bus.
3. The shops _____ (open, opens) at 10: O'clock each morning.
4. Anuradha _____ (have, had, has) a new bag.
5. Birds _____ (flow, flies, fly) in the air.
6. The postman _____ (brings, bring, brought) letters thrice a day.
7. Sunita and Sudha _____ (has, had, have) new mobile phones.
8. Jagriti _____ (be verb) a tall girl.
9. Raju, Sumit and Roshan _____ (is, are) good friends.
10. Many Children _____ (be) good players.

Present Continuous Tenses

Form of present continuous

Change in continuous tense

'Be' verbs is, are, am change into _____ being.

Has, have, is, are, am having (can't be used in every situation)

Do, does, is are, am doing

Action Verbs

Sing is, are, am singing

Clean is, are, am cleaning

Scold is, are, am, scholding

Wash is, are, am washing

Begin is, are, am beginning

Start is, are, am starting

Note: spelling rules

1. If a verb ends with 'e' this ending 'e' is dropped before putting – ing form of verb.

   Examples

   Write – writing

   Live - living

2. If the verb is of one syllable and it ends with a consonant preceded by a vowel, the consonant is doubled before

Adding 'ing'	step – stepping
Hit – hitting	drip – dripping
Run – running	cut – cutting
Stop – stopping	beg - begging

3. If the verb is of two or more syllables and the stress falls on the last syllable and ends with a consonant preceded by a vowel, the consonant is doubled before

   Ending – 'ing'

   Begin – beginning

TENSES

Admit – admitting

Vomit - vomitting

4. If the verb ends in a single 'l' preceded by a vowel, 'l' is doubled before adding – ing

   Quarrel   quarrelling
   Compel   compelling
   Signal   signalling

B. Exercise

Use the appropriate verbs in present continuous tense sit, clip, sip, admit, file, give, hit, put, dip, ride, slide, cry, smoke, smuggle, smile, compile, down, climb, run, trail

1. The child _____ (slide) his boat on snow.
2. I _____ (compile) my grammar manuscript in a book.
3. He _____ (cry) continuously, please see what his problem is.
4. The mountaineers _____ (climb) up the mountain.
5. Our teacher _____ (give) us our test papers.
6. The management has started _____ (admit) students.
7. Some people are enjoying _____ (sip) coffee.
8. Your face becomes pleasant while you _____ (smile)
9. The drug traffickers _____ (smuggle) drugs.
10. The naughty children _____ (hit) a dog.
11. The jockey _____ (ride) a horse.
12. The librarian _____ (put) the books on the shelf.
13. Father _____ (dip) his pen in the ink-pot.
14. Some people _____ (clip) the sheets of paper.

15. My daughter _____ (sit) beside me.
16. Dogs _____ after that deer. (run)
17. The sledge _____ (trail) behind the dogs.
18. The fire _____ (smoke) the room.

C. Exercise

Re-write the sentences given in Exercise 'B' in interrogative form and negative form.

Examples : The baby is crying.

1. Is the baby crying?
2. The baby is not crying.

   They are hiding in the forest.

   Are they hiding in the forest?

   They are not hiding in the forest.

D. Exercise

Fill in the blanks using simple present tense or present continuous tense of the given verbs.

1. The blind man _____ (has/have) a stick to get support on it.
2. The police (hide) in different locations to find the criminal.
3. Mothers always _____ (take) care of their children.
4. Aeroplanes _____ (fly) up in the sky.
5. My parents _____ (not live) in America.
6. Arun usually _____ (eat) from this dhaba.
7. The wounded soldier _____ (not has, not have, not having) any help.

TENSES

8. The road _____ (is having, has, have) ditches.
9. Priya _____ (not know) the answer.
10. The labourers _____ (carry) cement and bricks to the construction site.
11. Mother _____ (wash) clothes early in the morning.
12. Reema and Seema _____ (discuss) some secrets.
13. We _____ (see, sees, are seeing) stars shining at night.
14. People _____ (goes/go) to hill stations during summer. They _____ (not go) there when it _____ (be) cold but some _____ (visit, visits) hill stations when it _____ (snow).
15. I _____ (read) this book now.
16. Some guests _____ (leaving) today.
17. My aunt _____ (has, have, having) a lot of work to finish.
18. _____ you _____ (is, am, are, come) with me?
19. _____ she _____ (help, helps) the needy?
20. _____ (is, are, am) my name in that list?

Past Indefinite or Simple Past Tense

Forms in which verbs change into Simple Past and Past Participle form.

1. Rules – regular change of some verbs. They take – ed after the verb.

Present	Past	Past participle
Help	helped	helped
Cook	cooked	cooked
Work	worked	worked

2. Simple present tense of the verb changes indifferent ways.

Present	Past	Past Participle
Give	gave	given
Sit	sat	sat
Go	went	gone

3. These forms of verbs are the same.

Present	Past	Participle
Cut	cut	cut
Shut	shut	shut
Put	put	put
Let	let	let
Read	read	read
Set	set	set
Split	split	split
Cost	cost	cost
Burst	burst	burst

4. Two forms of verb are the same

Present	Past	Past Participle
Has, have	had	had
Hear	heard	heard
Bring	brought	brought
Hold	held	held
Come	came	come
Dream	dreamt./dreamed	dreamt/dreamed
Find	found	found
Feed	fed	fed
Dig	dug	dug
Feel	felt	felt
Beat	beat	beaten

Teach	taught	taught
Creep	crept	crept
Fly	flew	flown
Flow	flowed	flowed
Lay	laid	laid (transitive verb my sister lays the table for meals.).
Lie	Lay	Lain (intransitive verb - He lies down after lunch.) He has lain. (sleeps, rests)
Lie	lied	lied (He lies, He lied to me, He lied to them)
Stand	stood	stood
Strike	struck	struck
Win	won	won

5. Three forms are different

Present	**Past**	**Past Participle**
Fall	fell	fallen
Fly	flew	flown
Choose	chose	chosen
Drive	drove	driven
Drink	drank	drunk
Eat	ate	eaten
Blow	blew	blown
Fly	flew	flown
Strike	struck	stricken, struck
Wear	wore	worn
Write	wrote	written
Throw	threw	thrown

Note : Action verbs are numerous; Please consult the dictionary according to the needed form.

A. Exercise

Fill up the blanks using the verbs in simple past tense

1. The climbers _____ (fall) in the valley full of ice.
2. Shakespeare _____ (write) many popular poems.
3. The master _____ (feed) his pet dog.
4. The river _____ (flow) speedily.
5. Some people _____ (cut) the trees last year.
6. Sonal _____ (read) the book and enjoyed it
7. My ears pained because I _____ (hear) the blaring horn.
8. The birthday child _____ (blow) off the candles and the guests started clapping and singing.
9. As soon as Mr. Das _____ (strike) the match, the dry straw _____ (catch) fire and it _____ (spread) all over the area.
10. As soon as Mother _____ (lay) the table, she _____ (call) the family to have dinner.
11. Last Friday the guests _____ (eat) the delicacies.
12. Some people _____ (not throw) the garbage into proper bins.
13. The family _____ (not shut) the gate before going out.
14. The criminal _____ (lie) many times before.
15. How much _____ this car _____ (cost) five years ago.
16. Yesterday when he _____ (fill) the balloons with air, some _____ (burst).
17. A student _____ (not wear) school uniform so the incharge _____ (send) him back home.

18. Ajit _____ (drink) some juice and _____ (feel) refreshed.
19. They _____ (begin) the project late at night.
20. Ronit _____ (say) sorry to his mother for his misbehavior.

Simple Past Tense
B. Exercise

Rewrite the following sentences into interrogative and negative forms.

Structures of negative

Was not, were not, did not, had not

1. Children made noise.
2. The committee members were of the same point of view.

    1. a. Children didn't or did not make noise.
       b. Did the children make a noise\
    2. a. The committee members were not, weren't of the same point of view
       b. Were the committee member of the same opinion?
3. The captain ordered the players to get ready to play.
4. The farmer prepared the field to sow the seeds.
5. The soldiers were ready to attack.
6. Mohini lost her doll.
7. The swimmer dived into deep water.
8. The fish shop had variety of fish
9. Father was happy with his daughter's result.
10. My son did hard work.
11. The snake slithered into the hole

12. Our relatives came to meet us.
13. The teacher explained grammar rules clearly.
14. This bakery baked delicious snacks.
15. The policemen were alert.

Perfect Tenses
Present Perfect Tense
Work completed; spoken about it in the present time.
Structures has + past participle

Have + past participle
1. Has is used when the subject is third person singular pronoun or noun.

   Example : The carpenter + has made a beautiful table.
   He has spoken the truth.

2. 'Have' is used when plural pronouns or plural nouns are used. 'Have' is also used with subject 'I' and 'you'.

   Examples : These ladies + have cooked delicious dishes
   We + have completed the task.
   I + have bought some books.
   You + have done a wonderful job.

Note :
   a. The work done in the past, discussed in the present takes present perfect tense.

   Example : I have seen the Blue Nile Falls in Ethiopia.
   The writer saw them thirty years ago but recalling them now while I am writing this sentence.

TENSES

b. Present perfect tense can take adverbs like 'just', 'already'.

They have already resolved the problem.

The principal has just arrived

c. Present Perfect tense can be used in complex sentences to indicate the first action.

As; After I have prepared the doe, I will bake it.

Have prepared – first action

Will bake – second action

A. Exercise

Fill up the blanks using has + past participle or have + past participle

1. The plants _____ (grow) healthy
2. The mob _____ (become) destructive.
3. I _____ (blow) off the candle.
4. After the children _____ (sleep), Mother will clean the house.
5. I'm sorry, I can't watch this film as I _____ (see) it.
6. _____ you _____ (soak) those dirty clothes in hot soap water?
7. I'm sorry, the manager _____ (leave)
8. Together with my friends I _____ seen the Taj Mahal.
9. The company _____ (decide) to shift to the new office.
10. The shepherd _____ (take) the cattle to the grazing ground.

Note : Use 'since' if the starting time of an action is stated

Use 'for' if length of time is stated.

11. Mr. Singh _____ worked in this office _____ April, 209.
12. Arun _____ (plough) the field just _____ two hours and can't be seen anywhere.
13. That man _____ (stand) in front of that shop _____ quite a long time.
14. How long _____ you _____ (know) your Russian friends?
15. The Maliks _____ (live) in N.C.R _____ 1990.

B. Exercises

Write the following sentences in Interrogative and negative form.

1. The labourers have eaten their lunch.
2. The injured man has lain on the road for three hours.
3. The coolie has carried the heavy luggage.
4. The plumber has fixed the taps.
5. I have bought the ration from Easy Day.
6. Our pug, Candy has always shown her love to us.
7. The magician has mesmerized his audience.
8. The draper has sold a lot of clothes.
9. She has done her work.
10. The stationer has sold stationery.

Present Perfect Continuous Tense

Structure has + been + - ing form of the verb use _ since or for

Example : a. The baby has been sleeping since five p.m.
b. The police have been searching for the criminal for months.

C. Exercise

Complete the following sentences using present perfect continuous tense.

1. The storm _____ (blow) and the trees _____ (sway) to and from.
2. The frightened soldiers _____ (flee) from the battle field.
3. These people _____ (drink) palm wine as they are relaxing.
4. The cruel man _____ (kicking and beating) that poor dog heartlessly.
5. The sick tiger _____ (shiver) all these hours.
6. The poodle _____ (jump) over fences and bushes to reach his master.
7. The librarian _____ (arrange) the books on shelves since 9:30 a.m.
8. That lady _____ (spend) too much money on fads.
9. The jeweler _____ (earn) a lot of money but he is so kind that he doesn't shirk from helping the needy.
10. They _____ (keep) their windows open to let fresh air in.

Past Perfect Tense and Past Perfect Continuous

Had + Past participle = Past perfect

Example : I had notified the committee members about the meeting when the authorities told me to do so.

Had been + ing – past perfect continuous

D. Exercise

Change the given sentences into interrogative and negative form using past perfect and past perfect continuous tense.

1. The hunters had found the unique bird in the forest.
2. The guard had been watching the bank dutifully.
3. All the beds had been occupied by patients.
4. The photographers had been clicking the rioters' misdeeds.
5. The plane had taken off before kumars reached the airport.
6. The drummers had been making such a loud noise that none could hear each other.
7. After somebody had misled the doctor, the doctor became his prey.
8. The cat had killed the hen.
9. The players had played well.
10. Students had studied all the subjects before sitting for their exams.

Future Tense

1. Future Indefinite or Simple Future Tense

    'I' and 'we' take shall + simple present to show only 'future'.

    'I' and 'we' take 'will' to show future, threat, promise, order, determination.

2. All other nouns or pronouns take 'will' to show future. If used with 'shall' future, threat, promise, order, determination are shown.

A. Exercise

Fill in the blanks using 'will' or 'shall' according to the explanation given above. Use the clues correctly.

TENSES

1. He who comes late _____ be punished. (threat)
2. I _____ meet you at 9 a.m. (promise)
3. You _____ act according to my advice. (order)
4. We _____ win the match at all cost. (determination)
5. I _____ not meet him in any circumstances. (determination)
6. You _____ not get anything until you ask. (determination).
7. I _____ meet you next week if possible. (future)
8. They _____ come if they get time. (future)
9. I don't know if this tree _____ grow taller.
10. Amar _____ go to school as usual.

The underlined verbs also show simple future.

Note :

1. Simple present is used for official programmes as : The final exams **start** from February.
2. Plan for future.

    Mr. Singh **is going** to Sri Lanka next week. (present continuous tense)
3. Condition in the present indicates what will follow.

    It is dark with black clouds; it **is going** to rain.
4. The schools **are to be** inspected soon.

Study the given table

Group 1	Group 2	Group 3	Group 4
Simple Future	Future Continuous	Future Perfect	Future Perfect continuous

Will, shall play	Will, shall be playing	Will, shall have played	Will, shall have been playing
Will, shall cook	Will, shall be cooking	Will, shall have cooked	Will, shall have been cooking
Will, shall work	Will, shall be working	Will, shall have worked	Will, shall have been working

B. Exercise

Fill in the blanks using future tense of the given verbs according to the groups given above.

1. Malhotras _____ ('go' in future continuous) abroad by the end of this year.
2. By the end of this week, the mountaineers _____ (climb) up the peak (group 3).
3. I am sure our team _____ (win) the match.
4. Rahul _____ (compete) in that game.
5. The ladies Can't give you any time to group as they _____ (cook) special dishes for the eminent guests. (group 2)
6. By next June the novelist _____ (future perfect completed) his second novel.
7. By the end of four years, Rajan _____ still (serve) his term in the prison. (future continuous)
8. By the time the Sun sets we _____ (play) to our hearts' content. (future perfect)
9. By the time Sonu completes his studies his parents _____ (spend) a lot of money on his studies.
10. Anu _____ (take) the earliest bus to Agra.

11. They _____ (have) their lunch with me tomorrow.
12. One _____ (think) differently when one is an adult.
13. By 6 O'clock he _____ (clean) the campus for one hour.
14. The shopkeeper _____ (not let) you go unless you make the full payment.
15. They _____ (live) in Delhi for ten years when Mr. Das retires.
16. By this time tomorrow Anoop _____ (search) the reception venue.
17. Don't be worried, your friend _____ (recover) soon.
18. _____ they be investigating the crime?
19. Are you sure if they _____ (take) you to Nainital.
20. Tomorrow we _____ (have) some delicacies.

C. Exercise

Recapitulation of tenses as a whole

1. He _____ (fight) like a mad man when he _____ (challenge) his opponent.
2. I _____ (be) happy to attend your birthday party.
3. When I first met him, he _____ (attend) some extra courses.
4. Somebody _____ (knock) on the door for the last ten minutes.
5. John _____ (not play) in the match as his foot was injured.
6. Seema wrote to her two months ago but she _____ (not reply) yet.
7. _____ you _____ (see) the film that is shown at the Regal?

8. They _____ (have) difference of opinion in the past and _____ (be) on bad terms ever since.
9. When he _____ (employ), he _____ (get) free medical support.
10. If her husband _____ (be) alive, she _____ (not suffer) so much.
11. If the judge _____ (not sentence) her to death, she will kill herself.
12. Sahel _____ (learn) French for the past five years but he can't speak it.
13. I _____ (wait) for the bus since 7 a.m., I am so exhausted that I can't keep on standing any more.
14. I _____ (study) your proposal. I'm sorry, I can't accept it.
15. He usually _____ (leave) office at 6:00 p.m. but this week he _____ (have) to work for more hours.
16. Today the labourers _____ (sit) under a tree and _____ (relax) as they have completed most of the work.
17. Robert _____ (be) very happy because his exams _____ (be) over.
18. Children _____ (play) in the park every day.
19. An ambulance _____ (passing) by and the students _____ (run) out.
20. The master of these donkeys _____ (sleep) while these animals _____ (carry) heavy loads on their backs.
21. Some students _____ (throw) chits of paper while the teacher _____ (write) on the black board.
22. We _____ (be) eating oranges but they _____ (be) eating apples.

TENSES

23. I _____ (have, has) a lot of work to do but he (not have) anything to do.
24. Lions _____ (eat, eats) _____ (meet, meat); deer _____ (eat, eats) grass.

Edit the following sentences. One word is wrong in each sentence. Write the, wrong word on the left and correct word on the right side of the given dashes.

1

The small child have eaten.	a.	_____ _____
many biscuits so he is cry.	b.	_____ _____
His parent are taking him	c.	_____ _____
to doctor. I hope he will got	d.	_____ _____
well soon. His grand – mother	e.	_____ _____
seem to be very much worried	f.	_____ _____

2

I go to a hill station last year.	a.	_____ _____
It is very cold.	b.	_____ _____
We forget to take woolens	c.	_____ _____
With us so we catch cold.	d.	_____ _____
I have high temperature	e.	_____ _____
Cough and cold. It become difficult	f.	_____ _____
For I to breathe.	g.	_____ _____

3

Find the missing word. Write it between two correct words

My children gone to school.	a. _____ _____ _____
They will back at noon.	b. _____ _____ _____
I give your message to them.	c. _____ _____ _____
If I not at home, I will leave	d. _____ _____ _____
The message at home. They get	e. _____ _____ _____
It. Please not worry.	f. _____ _____ _____

MAIN CLAUSES & SUBORDINATE CLAUSES

A. Time Clauses

The connectors, after, before, till, until, when, while are used in time clause

When

Two actions simultaneous

A. In the present

Structure: Subordinate clause simple present tense, main clause simple future tense

Example: Subordinate clause Main clause

When I pinch him, he will wake up with a start.

Exercise

Complete the following sentences using correct form of the given verbs:

1. When it ------------ [start] raining, I ---------- [take] out my umbrella.
2. when I -------- [pull] her hair, she ------- [turn] back.
3. This balloon -------- [burst] when you ------- [poke] it with a pin.
4. You ------- [pull] back your hand when you -------- [touch] this hot pan.

5. He --------- [come] out of his house when he ------- [hear] you.
6. Renu ---------- [jump] with excitement when she ----------- [come] to know the good news.
7. Mother -------- [shout] at you when she ------- [see] the broken dishes.
8. When the bell ---------- [ring], the invigilator ---------- [tell] the students to start writing.
9. When the guard ------ [wave] the red flag, the train -------- [start] moving.
10. When Sarla ------------ [eat] hot food, she --------- [drink] water with each bite.

B. Two simultaneous actions in the past

Structure: Subordinate clause simple past, main clause simple past

Example: When the door suddenly slammed, she jumped up in alarm.

Exercise

Complete the following sentences to show that two actions were almost simultaneous in the past.

1. When the plane -------- [catch] fire, the crew --------[parachute] to safety.
2. When orientation -------- [be] over, the students --------- [go] to their classroom.
3. When they ----------[mow] the lawn, the mower --------- [make] a lot of noise.
4. When I -------- [push] him, he -------- [turn] back.
5. Tom --------- [get] angry when Joan --------[snatch]his notebook.

CLAUSES

7. The passengers ---------- [serve] soft drinks when the plane -------- [take] off.
8. They-----------[run]into their house when they -------- [hear] gun shots.
9. When she -------- [put] the tablet in her mouth, she ------- [spit] it out.

Present perfect goes with simple future
Exercise

Use one verb in present perfect tense to show that this action took place before the second action.

1. When I **have written** [write] the letter, I **will pass** [pass] it on to you to add something more to it.
2. When she -------- [mop] the house, she --------[take] a bath.
3. They ---------[eat] mangoes when they --------- (wash) them.
4. The nurse -------- [give] the injection to the patient when she --------- [instruct]to do so by the doctor.
5. The farmer --------- [sow] seeds when he --------- [plough] the field.
6. The conductor ---------- [check] our tickets when we all -------- [take]our seats.
7. When you ---------- [complete] all the formalities, you ---------- [allow]to leave the country.
8. When the team---------- [win] the game, it -------- [award].

In the past
Structure:

Subordinate clause simple past, main clause simple past

When the match ended, the players went for a hot shower

Exercise

Complete the following sentences using correct form of the given verbs.

1. When the epidemic----------- [bring] under control, the medical staff----------[breath] a sigh relief.
2. When the workers-------- [dig] the ground, they------------ [lay] the foundation.
3. I---------- [feel] much better when I----------- [drink] that medicine
4. He--------- [start] to sing and shout when he ----------- [take] too much alcohol.
5. They----------- [sit] down to eat when all the guests-------- [arrive]

Exercise

Complete the following sentences using past perfect tense to identify the first action

Example:

When the match had ended, the players went for a hot shower.

1. When I ---------- (write) the letter, I ------------ (post) it.
2. Mother ------------ (rest) when she ------ (do) all the work.
3. Sohan -------- (take) the exam when he ------------- (study) well.
4. He ----------- (submit) the report when he -------------- (go) through all the details.
5. when they ----------- (collect) all the dirt, they ---------- (put) it into a dust bin.
6. I---- (go) off to sleep when I --------- (make) my bed.

Time clauses with while

Two parallel continuous actions in the past

Example

    A.   While we were sleeping, the thief ransacked our house.

    B.   While we were sleeping, the thief was ransacking the house.

Exercise

Complete the following sentences using structure A and B.

1. While the rain -------- [pour] down, the children -------- [amuse] themselves on the verandah
2. While Mother -------- [cook] the food, we [do] our homework
3. The farmer -------- [plough] the field while her son ------- [break] the lumps of soil.
4. Kamala -------- [pass] a chit around while the teacher ------ [teach].
5. While Sam ------- [read] the newspaper, John ------ [paint] the scenery.
6. While Enid ------ [write] the manuscript, Michael --------- [attend] a meeting.
7. The mason ---------- [repair] the house while the laborers --------- [carry] the building material.
8. While we -------- [visit] the monuments, some friends of ours --------- [rest].

In the present time

One short action interrupting an action of longer duration in the present time

Structure
Example:
While the sun is shining, I will hang out the clothes.

Exercise
Complete the following sentences to show that a short action is interrupting an action of longer duration in the present time.

1. While the children---------- [rest], I------- [tidy] up the room.
2. While you ---------- [chat] with your friends, I --------- [write] a letter.
3. I----------- [prepare] tea while you---------- [watch] the film.
4. Two of the men ------------ [keep] the things in the tent while one--------- (sleep).
5. While it---------- [rain], we---------- [play] some music.

In the past
Structure:
While + longer action past continuous tense, short action + simple past

Example:
While the surgeon was operating, the nurse entered the theatre.

Exercise
Complete the following sentences according to the given structure to show a short action interrupted a longer action in the past

1. while he---------- [reverse] the car out of the narrow gateway, he--------- [bump] into the gate.
2. Somebody ------- [knock] on the door while we --------- [sleep]

CLAUSES

3. While the cleaning campaign ----------- [go] on, the principal --------- [arrive].
4. While the kites--------- [fly] up in the sky, they -------- [hear] a gun shot.
5. A lady ------- [faint], while the magician ------- [show] tricks.

Frequent or repeated actions with adverbs like often, generally, usually, always

In the present
Structure:
While preset continuous, simple present

Example:
While I am taking a nap, you always come and make a lot of noise.

Exercise
Complete the given sentences according to the given structure.

1. The baby usually ------- [cry] while she ------- [have] her hair trimmed.
2. They generally--------- [wear] shorts while they-------- [play] games.
3. While I ----------- [work] in the garden my son usually ------------ [come] to help me in the weeding.
4. She always---------- [keep] the windows and doors shut while she----------- [spray] the house.
5. I often --------- [sing] while I----------- [do] odd jobs around the house.
6. That shopkeeper often-------- [try] to cheat you while you------- [shop] at his store.

'After and Before'

'After' in the present time

Structure

After + present perfect, simple future

'Before' in the present time

Structure

Before + simple present, simple future

Example: a.   After she has left the dough to rise for twenty minutes, she will put it in the oven to bake.
b.   Before she puts the dough in the oven to bake, she will leave it to rise for twenty minutes.

Note: the subordinate clause which begins with 'after' changes into main clause and the main clause takes '**before**' so it changes into subordinate clause

Exercise

A. Complete the following sentences using present perfect and simple future tense of the given verbs correctly.

B. Rewrite the completed sentences using 'before'

1. After they ---------- [study] the whole situation thoroughly, they -------- [discuss] it with the governing body.
2. After the children ------ [wash] their hands, they ----- [help] me to dry up the dishes.
3. After the director ------- [sign] the form, he-------- [give]it to the dean.
4. After you ------- [cook] the onions thoroughly, you-------- [add] butter.

CLAUSES

5. After the painter [apply] a lead base to the wood, he --------[put]on the finishing coat of oil paint.
6. After the campaigners -------- [dig] a small hole and ------- [fill]it with water, they-------[plant the seedlings].

After and Before in the past time
Structure
After past perfect, simple past

Before simple past, simple past

Example
After he had put on his reading glasses, he picked up the newspaper.

Before he picked up the newspaper, he put on his reading glasses.

Exercise
Complete the following sentences using past perfect tense and simple past tense of the given verbs and then rewrite the completed sentences using 'before'.

1. After the fire ------- [spread] to the neighbourig house, the firemen finally------ [arrive].
2. After his father ------- [make] him promise to be careful, Michael ------ [be allow] to take the car out.
3. After the woodsmen---------- [mark] the trees carefully, they------- [cut] them down.
4. After the chairman ------- [prepare] his speech, he ------- [deliver] it to the Youth Association at their Saturday meeting.
5. After the team ------- [take] their positions, the game ------ [begin].

Exercise

Fill in the blanks with suitable words given below:

As soon as, till, until, as long as, for, since

1. I will be holding this office only --------the end of this month.
2. We have been neighbours --------1993.
3. _____ you are on the right path, no one can harm you.
4. Children ran out of their classrooms---------the bell rang.
5. I have taught in this school-------twenty-three years.
6. The labourers have been carrying stones-----------11:30 a.m.
7. you can stay here------you want.
8. They were with us----------4 o' clock.
9. _____ Mohan saw the principal coming, he ran into the classroom
10. Uncle hasn't written to us------------- September.

Adverb Phrases of Purpose

Adverb phrases of purpose indicate purpose in a sentence.

Phrase is a group of words which cannot be divided into subject and predicate; it doesn't give complete sense

Purpose phrases take conjunctions to, in order to, so as to

Example :

They have gone out **to see the procession**

They have gone out **in order to see the procession**.

They have gone out **so as to see the procession**.

Exercise

Join the following sentences using the given conjunctions:

1. She is studying day and night. She wants to pass with good marks.
2. Charles left home early. He wanted to see off his friends at the air –port.
3. Helen is preparing some especial programme. She wants to entertain the guests.
4. Father has taken some money from mother. He wants to buy a pair of shoes.
5. She is walking fast. She wants to catch up with her friends.

Clauses of purpose In the present

Clauses of purpose take the conjunctions so that, in order that, lest, for fear

Structure

Notice verb agreement in both the clauses

A. simple present tense goes with can or will, form of present tense

Examples

A. She **cooks** fast so that she **doesn't spend** a lot of time in the kitchen She **is cooking** fast so that she **can watch** the t.v. programme.
B. They will leave early in order that they can catch the train.
C. The teacher **has left** home early so that she **can discuss** certain points with the principal before the meeting.

Exercise:

Arrange the jumbled parts correctly and join them with the given sentences using the connectors so that or in order that to supply purpose clauses.

1. I'll give you my telephone number. you me telephone

   Answer: I'll give you my telephone number so that you can telephone me.
2. He has bought a new dictionary. look up the words he
3. There is a radio telephone. the can captain the contact shore base
4. They are going to put in new furniture. you comfortable be
5. The captain is not paying attention to any other thing. He not want time waste
6. The participants will be called again. they collect awards their
7. Workers are going on strike. wages their increase
8. Uncle takes morning walk. feel he fresh the whole day
9. She is sending the money order today. get her mother soon it
10. The tourists will carry their cameras with them. take they photographs.

Purpose Clauses in the Past
Structure:
Simple past would or could + infinitive

Example:
They used loud speakers, so that everyone could hear.

CLAUSES

Note : When the purpose shows desire, use would + infinitive
When the purpose means ability, use could + infinitive
'Want' indicates desire or wish; 'could' indicates ability

Exercise:

Join the following pairs of sentences using so that or in order that.

1. He moved closer. He wanted to read the message.

   Answer: He moved closer so that he would read the message.

2. The driver changed the gear. He wanted to go round the corner slowly.
3. Our neighbours went to Shimla by air. They wanted to reach there before it got dark.
4. I got a ladder. My son was able to get the cat down from the tree.
5. He brought baking powder. His wife would be able to bake cake.
6. The farmer used new scientific methods. He wanted to get a better crop.

Purpose Clauses in negative form

Note:

Present tense agrees with affirmative or negative form of can, will+ infinitive

Past tense agrees with affirmative or negative form of could, would + infinitive

If purpose shows wish, will or would are used. If it shows ability, use could or couldn't.

Exercise

Join the following sentences using so that or in order that; change the second sentence into negative purpose clause.

1. He built a wall around the campus. He didn't want the neighbours to destroy his garden.

   Answer: He built a wall around the campus so that the neighbours wouldn't destroy his garden.
2. They created a din. They didn't want the speaker to be heard.
3. They turned their faces. They didn't want to see the tragic scene.
4. She keeps disturbing the auditor. She doesn't want him to detect the errors.
5. The driver is changing the route. The rogues aren't able to follow him.
6. He carried the vase carefully. He didn't want it to break.
7. The policeman stood very still. He didn't want to be heard.
8. The child crawled under the bed. He didn't want to be seen.
9. She keeps a door mat at the threshold. She doesn't want the people to dirty the house.
10. Thomas is hiding the answers. Students aren't able to cheat from him.
11. The victim is blind folded. He is not able to see the criminals.
12. The lights were put off. The thieves were able to break into the house

Purpose Clause with 'lest' and 'for fear'

When the purpose shows fear, the subordinate clause takes 'lest' or 'for fear'. They both have the same meaning. The subordinate clause can take may, might, shall, or should +infinitive

Exercise

Answer the following questions using lest or for fear. Use the words given in the brackets.

1. Why were the schools closed? [riots]

   Answer: The schools were closed lest or for fear there might be riots.
2. Why did they keep quiet? [punish]
3. Why did farmers harvest the wheat earlier? [rain]
4. Why did they take water with them? [thirsty]
5. Why did he hide under the bed?[beat]
6. Why did the accused tear the proof? [catch]
7. Why did Tom climb up the tree? [catch]
8. Why did he twist her hand? [slap] him.

Adverb Clauses of Result

These clauses indicate the result of some prior happening, situation or condition.

Example:

The labourer is so tired that he can't climb up the top floor.

Result can be for present, future or past situations.

Conjunctions used for result clauses are so------that, such-----that, (too----to, too----for – They show faces of result.

Structure:

Note the verb agreement

He is so nervous that he can't give the interview properly.

He will be so nervous that he won't give the interview properly.

Mr.Stanly was so restless that he didn't sleep the whole night.

He was so restless that he couldn't sleep the whole night.

He was so restless that he wouldn't enjoy the magic show.

Exercise:
Purpose Clauses in the present

Complete the following sentences in the present situation.

1. The sums -------[be] so difficult that the students ------[not solve] them

   Answer: the sums are so difficult that the students can't solve them.

2. There----[be] so much noise in the neighbourhood that I -------[not sleep] at all.

3. The road ------ [be]------- flooded that traffic-------[not move] smoothly.

4. Whenever help is needed, she ------[act] so indifferently that nobody -----[dare] to come forward to ask for her help.

5. He ---------[walk] so slowly that he -------[not catch]up with the group going ahead.

6. Jerry ------[dress] up so clumsily that he ------[look] so shabby.

7. That class --------[make] so much noise that we---------[not listen]to the teacher.

Result Clauses in the past
Exercise

Change the following sentences into past form:

1. Rahul has become so weak that he can't resume his work.

   Answer: Rahul had become so weak that he couldn't resume his work.

2. The room is so dirty that I can't stay here anymore.

3. She works so slowly that she can never finish her work on time.

4. They have so many visitors that they can't attend to each properly.
5. The food is so delicious that I want to keep on eating.
6. The book is so interesting that I can't leave it.
7. These instructions are so complicated that we can't follow them.
8. The film is so boring that I have to switch it off.

Exercise:

Rewrite the following sentences using too----to or too---for sentences

Note: if the subjects of two clauses are different, use too---for; if the subjects are the same, use too---to structure. Replace so by too and that by 'to' or 'for'.

Example:

That boy is so young that he can't become a soldier.

Answer: That boy is too young to become a soldier.

The road is so slippery that we can't go further.

Answer: The road is too slippery for us to go further.

1. The boy is so short that he can't reach that fruit.
2. You are so heavy that she can't lift you up.
3. Daniel is so young that he can't shoulder his father's responsibilities as yet.
4. This food is so hot that children can't relish it.
5. The suitcase was so expensive that we couldn't purchase it.
6. I am so helpless that I can't help you.
7. The mango is so sour that I can't eat it any more.

8. She is so dull that she can't follow even these lessons.
9. The wind was so strong that the boat couldn't be controlled.
10. Team 'A' is so slow that it can't win the game.

Exercise:

Rewrite the following sentences using so---that structure. The verbs in two clauses should match with each other.

1. He is too short to arrange this stuff on the upper shelf.

   Answer: He is so short that he can't arrange this stuff on the upper shelf.
2. Rao is too weak to go about his daily routine.
3. Madhuri was too frightened to speak.
4. These poems are too deep that light readers can't enjoy them.
5. Renu spoke too softly to be heard.
6. Olive is too weak to bear this harsh treatment.
7. The playground is too far for this young boy to reach there on time.
8. Your story was too ridiculous to be believed.
9. The criminals were too ruthless to deserve any pity.
10. He is too clever to be caught.

Result Clause with 'such---that'

Note: Structures of 'so' and 'such' differ.

Example

This car is so expensive that he can't afford it. **(Right)**

This is so expensive car that he can't afford it. **(wrong)**

CLAUSES

'So' can't be followed by adjective + noun.

This is such an expensive car that he can't afford it. **(Right)**

Exception to the rule

1. There are so <u>few</u> students in the class that I can't take the lesson I planned. Sentences with **'few'** can't take **'such'**.
2. You have made so many mistakes that your rank will come down.
3. There is so much salt in this curry that no one will relish it.
4. There is so little money that she can't buy all the things listed.

Such structures are possible only with the determiners few, many, much, little.

Structure of 'such' takes an adjective + a noun.

This is such an expensive car that he can't afford it.

Rewrite the following sentences using such----that

Some changes will be necessary.

Exercise:

1. Those shoes are so uncomfortable that Tom can't wear them.

   Those are such uncomfortable shoes that Tom can't wear them.

2. This vase is so fragile that it can't be handled with negligence.
3. This route is so long that we can't reach our destination on time.
4. The task is so complicated that we can't work it out easily.

5. The grapes are so sour that we can't eat them.
6. The knife is so blunt that I can't chop these onions.
7. These colours are so dull that they don't attract children.
8. He speaks so boldly that it is difficult to make his audience agree with him.
9. The food is so delicious that I want to keep on eating.
10. David is so polite that everyone likes him.

Practice exercise:

Fill in the blanks with 'so' or 'such':

1. He is _____ lazy that he can never come to office on time.
2. The food is _____ watery that it has lost its taste.
3. We have _____ few members that we can't form the club.
4. It is _____ old bicycle that no one wants it.
5. This is _____ sweet tea that I can't drink it.
6. It is _____ mysterious disease that doctors find it difficult to find its cure.
7. This is _____ steep climb that the climbers can't climb it.
8. He is _____ helpless that he can't guide you.
9. This is _____ unique idea that everyone will accept it.
10. There are _____ rats in this area that we can't get rid of them easily.
11. You have given us _____ clues that they can't help us easily.

CLAUSES

12. Eagles have -------------- keen eyes that they can't miss their prey.
13. The bandits follow _____ tricky hide-outs that the police can't trap them easily.
14. Mother is _____ good in household duties that no one can compete with her.
15. This safe has_____ complicated lock that outsiders cannot unlock it.

Adverb Clauses of reason

Reason clauses take the connectors because, as, since, for, seeing that, now that, considering that.

Exercise:

Join the following sentences using reason clauses:

1. She can't read. She hasn't put on her glasses.

    Answer: She can't read because she hasn't put on her glasses.

    Because she hasn't put on her glasses, she can't read.

2. You can't enter the examination hall. You are very late.
3. They couldn't finish the work on time. They were whiling away their time in gossiping.
4. He rang up his father. He had some important news to give.
5. I am glad. You like it.
6. She wasn't there. I couldn't inform her about the meeting.
7. He is very pleased. You have passed in the examination.
8. You have come. We can start the meeting.
9. I bought the dress. I liked it.

10. You are needed to serve me faithfully. I will employ you.
11. She called me. She wanted to tell me about the tragedy.
12. We can't miss the train. We'll reach the station much earlier.
13. He is sick. He won't come to school.
14. The brakes are out of order. We have to get them repaired.
15. He started the treatment late. His recovery won't be fast.
16. We are getting late. We can't wait for them any longer.
17. She opened her shoelaces. Her shoes were very tight.
18. He was paid much below his expectation. He left the job in frustration.
19. Amrita dances gracefully. She has been selected to perform on the Annual Day.
20. You will not be taken out. You misbehaved in front of the guests.

Participle Phrases used instead of Reason Clauses

Exercise:

Rewrite the following sentence using participle phrases:

1. Because he saw the door open, he came in.

   Answer: Seeing the door open, he came in.

2. Now that he has made the point clear, he can proceed.

   Answer: Having made the point clear, he can proceed.

3. Now that I have studied the whole situation, I can take proper steps.
4. As he was injured so badly, his recovery became remote.
5. Because he is very weak, he can't join his duties for some more time.

CLAUSES

6. Since he had spent all the money, he couldn't foot the electric bill.
7. Because you are guilty, you have to bear the consequences.
8. As he has played brilliantly, he will be awarded.

Practice Exercise:

Fill in the blanks using the connectors so, such, to, in order to, so that, In order that, too, because, as, since, enough, lest, for fear, in order

1. He is driving fast ------to reach there on time.
2. They left him behind--------they wanted to discuss something.
3. Students have started to run------they can reach school on time.
4. You are ------tricky to be caught easily.
5. Raju took a book with him------he wanted to read while traveling.
6. Jane took a book with her-------she could read while traveling.
7. I was tired ------I went to bed.
8. These mangoes are ------sour that we can't eat them.
9. Papayas are ripe -------to eat.
10. This scene is -------tragic that none could hold back tears.
11. The soup is --------salty that I can't drink it.
12. I went to him-------I could discuss some of the problems.
13. This scene is ---------heart breaking that nobody can hold back his tears.
14. The soup is --------salty that I can't drink it.
15. I went to him ----------I could discuss some of my problems with him.

Adjective Clauses

Adjective clauses begin with relative adjective or relative pronoun who, whom, which, whose, that, when, where, why

Example:

The man who had stolen my watch was caught.

Exercise:

Join the following sentences using adjective clauses.

1. The librarian fined the boy. He had not returned the books.
2. The girl carried the medal. She stood first.
3. The schools closed on this day for summer vacation. It was on May 15th.
4. The man handles cash in a company. He must be very careful.
5. My parents gifted me a pair of ear-rings. They are precious to me.

Relative pronouns can be in nominative case[subject] form or in accusative case[object] form.

How are the relative pronouns working

The girl who ranked first is my cousin. The relative pronoun is in nominative case.

Analysis :

A. The girl is my cousin.
B. Who ranked first.

In clause A 'the girl' is the subject.

In clause b 'who' is the subject referring to the subject 'girl' hence 'who' is in the nominative case.

The book which I bought yesterday is quite expensive. The relative pronoun 'which' is in the accusative case[object] form.

Analysis:

a. The book is quite expensive.

b. I bought the book the book yesterday

In clause 'a' the book is subject; in clause 'b' the book is object. Since 'which' is used for the object 'book'; the relative pronoun 'which' is in the accusative case[object form]. In such a sentence the relative pronoun can be retained or omitted.

Example:

The book which I bought yesterday is quite expensive.

The book I bought yesterday is quite expensive.

Defining or restrictive clauses

Such relative clauses are not separated by commas.

He gave me the book which he had bought recently.

He gave me the book that he had bought recently.

The relative clause 'which he had bought recently' is defining clause; it is essential as it specifies 'the book'; the given relative pronoun can be omitted.

We can say: He gave me the book he had bought recently.

The word 'that' can replace relative pronouns used in restrictive clauses.

Non – Defining or Non-Restrictive Clauses

The Taj Mahal, which is a monument, is in Agra.

Commas are needed to separate the relative clause the main clause is sufficient to give complete meaning.

Exercise:

Join the following sentences using the given clues:

1. The teacher is talking to the director. He suggested to start the debating club.[who suggested]
2. You saw the letter. I wrote it last night.[that]
3. You know the boy.I gave the packet to him.[to whom]
4. Rashmi saw the note. The note referred to the accident. [which]
5. Rekha threw away the rose.I gave it to her.[which]
6. Sarita didn't return the pen. I lent it to her.[which]
7. The headmaster is to meet the higher authorities. He will suggest reduction in fees.Begin with 'The head master-who'
8. The town is far away from the sea.He lives in the town. [begin with 'The town]
9. I can't forget the day. A man came to school drunk. [when]
10. Last summer the weather was pleasant. We spent our vacations in Shimla.[where]
11. This is the reason. I didn't entertain them.[why]
12. They gave away the clothes. They didn't need the clothes. [which]
13. The lady wrote this book.The lady is coming here today. [who]
14. You borrowed a book from me. Have you read the book?[begin with have—which]
15. He worked in a factory.It closed down last month. [which]
16. The road passed through a tunnel. The tunnel is two kilometer long.[which]

CLAUSES

17. I spent my holidays with the friend. The friend is coming tomorrow.[with whom]
18. The group will be leaving tomorrow for Bombay. They will stay there for a month.[which]
19. Mr. Kumar spoke in the end. He was the bese speaker. [who]
20. This is the house. We lived in it last year.[in which]
21. The boy was knocked down by a car yesterday. His condition is critical.[whose]
22. I am to do this work. It will take a lot of time.[which]
23. Cricket is played in several countries. It is a most popular game.[which]
24. The traveler was shot with a gun. The police have taken the gun. [with which]
25. These poems were written by a young poet. He passed away recently.[by whom]

Adverb Clauses of Comparison
Example
Rahul is as tall as his brother.

The given sentence can be written in other ways as well.

    a.   Rahul and his brother are the same in height.
    b.   The height of Rahul is the same as that of his brother.
    c.   Rahul is the same in height as his brother.
    d.   Rahul is as tall as if not more so than his brother.

Exercise:
Rewrite the following sentences according to the examples given above

1. This road is as wide as that one.
2. Sam is as tall as his sister.
3. The depth of this well is the same as that of the well in that field.
4. This route is as long as that one.
5. Your book is as thick as mine.
6. The soup in the white bowl is as tasty as the soup in the pink bowl.
7. The brown sofa set is as costly as the white sofa set.
8. This suitcase is as heavy as that

Exercise :

Fill in the blanks using suitable connectors and other changes neededT:

as-----as, that, so---as, no less than, as if not, more so than, as, the----the, as though, as if

1. ------you sow -----shall you reap.
2. He is ----tall ----I am.
3. -------higher you go ------cooler it gets.
4. You are not -------fat -------your brother.
5. The leader was -------kind -----polite.
6. You may do -----you please.
7. He looks the same ------you.
8. Mr. Thomas is cleverer ------his wife.
9. She acted------------she were mad.
10. Rahel is younger--------she looks.
11. No other exercise is ----------healthy--------walking.
12. Ramesh is --------[fast] than Mohan.

CLAUSES

13. Reena is --------[intelligent] than her sister.
14. That road is-------[wide] -------this one.
15. This room is ---------- [congested]---------that one.
16. I am not ----------happy-------she is.
17. The red car is --------attractive-------the blue one.
18. This tree bears ---------fruit-------that one.

Exercise:

Join the following sentences; use both the clues in two different sentences; if there is one clue, make one sentence:

1. Sarita is smart. Ashwini is smarter.[as---as, than]
2. Anita is intelligent. Seema is more intelligent.[less-than, more---than]
3. Your father is industrious. My father is more industrious. [as---as]
4. John works fast. You work fast.[as----as]
5. Narender fought courageously. Sameer fought less courageously.[more----than, less-----than]
6. Asha speaks English more fluently. Amar speaks English less fluently.[than]
7. Your dog is ferocious. My dog is not ferocious like yours. [as------as]
8. Renuka dresses up clumsily. Her friend dresses up less clumsily.[less, more]
9. It is not large. I thought it was large.[as----as, less---than]
10. It is very large. I thought it was not so large.[larger]
11. This climb is very steep. That climb is also very steep. [as--------as]
12. Your plan is convenient to me. Her plan is not so convenient to me.

Noun Clauses

Noun clauses have the same function as nouns have.

Noun clauses work like subject or object.

Example:

Example: I know that he is right.

The clause 'that he is right' has come after the verb 'know'; therefor, it is object to the verb know.

Why did he leave so early is not known to me.

The clause 'Why did he leave so early' has come before the verb 'is'; therefore, it is the subject of the verb 'is'.

Note the following structures:

Do you remember when they came? The first clause can be in the interrogative form.

Do you remember when did they come? This sentence is wrong because both the clauses have interrogative structure.

I know how he behaves in such situations.

I know how does he behave in such situations. This sentence is wrong because the second clause has interrogative structure. Both the clauses should have statement structure.

Exercise:

Write the wrong sentences correctly.

1. How can I know where has she gone?
2. Did you know why did he behave so rudely?
3. Is it certain that he will be able to solve this problem?
4. Are you aware what trouble can you face?
5. We know how did they cross the river?
6. I can guess which path they took.
7. She knows how should she cook this food.

CLAUSES

8. My parents understand why did my sister score such low marks.
9. Does Renu know where does your sister leave her books?
10. Do you know which book did your friend tear?

Noun clauses begin with the connectors that, if, whether, how, how much, how many, when, where, why, what, who, whom, which, whose

Join the following sentences using noun clauses with the given connectors:

1. The decision is that he should give up his studies. It is not a wise one. [Begin with The decision]
2. What does the Holy Book say? Listen to it.[begin with Listen]
3. God wills some thing. That is certain to happen.[begin with What]
4. I should do this sum. I don't know how.[begin with, I don' know]
5. I was right. The teacher told me so.[that]
6. The beggar was overjoyed. He had got a five Rupee coin. [over joyed that]
7. I said something. I meant it.[what]
8. He said something. It is of no importance to me.[what]
9. He is dead drunk. Everybody is saying so.[that]
10. You took away my pen. I knew it.[that]
11. Death is sudden. Everyone knows it.[that]
12. Birds know the danger of electric wires. It is interesting to know this.[that]
13. The accused was not guilty. The jury declared this.[This]
14. He begs something. He lives on it. [what]

15. Many died when the bridge collapsed. The report is untrue. [begin with the report]
16. He became a criminal. I could not understand. [how]
17. A wonderful change had come over us. Everyone noticed. [begin with everyone----- when]
18. The station is very far from here. Who told you this? [that]
19. The girl was blind in one eye. The report was spread by her enemies. [that]
20. All was well. He thought this. [that]

Clauses of Concession or Contrast

Subordinate concession or contrast clauses begin with conjunctions though, although, even though, despite the fact that, in spite of the fact that

Exercise :

Join the following sentences using the subordinating conjunctions of contrast or concession given above.

Example :

He sits at the back. He is always attentive.

    a. Although he sits at the back, he is always attentive.
    b. Though he sits at the back, he is always attentive.
    c. Even though he sits at the back, he is always attentive.
    d. In spite of the fact that he sits at the back, he is always attentive.
    e. Despite the fact that he sits at the back, he is always attentive.

Exercise :

Join the given pairs of sentences using though, although, even though, though- yet

1. It was very hot. They kept on marching.
2. He is very young. He is very mature in his behavior.
3. Father came in quietly. The baby woke up.
4. Mary's answer was right. her answer was marked wrong.
5. The food was delicious. My friend didn't relish it.
6. Mr. Thomas is very old. He participated in the races.
7. He was neither warned nor punished. He was very rude to the teacher.
8. The group reached the station on time. They missed the train.
9. Mohan ate the fruit. It smelled horrible.
10. He looked at me. He showed as if he didn't know me.
11. Tom was the youngest competitor. He was the first one to reach the top of the mountain.
12. Mamta played the music softly. The neighbours objected to it.
13. The patient recovered. His treatment was very costly.
14. The farmer used clean seeds. He didn't get a good crop.
15. The garbage was dumped in a proper place. The dogs scattered it.
16. I shouted her name. She didn't turn back.
17. The tree was given good care. It didn't yield fruit.

Exercise :

Join the given sentences using in spite of or despite.

Structure :

In spite of or despite + possessive adjective or possessive pronoun + -ing form [gerund]

Possessive adjectives are my, her, his, your, their, our

Possessive nouns can be formed from common nouns or proper nouns – girl's, girls';

teacher-teacher's, teachers – teachers'; Mohan's, Tom 's

Example :

He came on time. He was punished.

In spite of his coming on time, he was punished.

1. He worked hard. He didn't succeed.
2. She attended driving lessons. She couldn't pass the driving test.
3. She has had several cooking lessons. She can't cook well.
4. He is weak in studies. He doesn't care to pay attention to his studies.
5. They were rude to me. I had no grudges against them.
6. They have been trying for several hours. They haven't caught any fish so far.
7. I am listening to each word. I can't get what he really means.

Note: If the principal clause has only one verb, it changes into –ing form.

In spite of his telling the truth, he was severely punished. 'Told' has been changed into 'telling '.

Was, were, is, are, am change into 'being'. She is weak yet she does all her work diligently.

Despite being weak, she does her work diligently.

Have and has change into having.

I am going home because I have completed my work.

Having completed my work, I am going home.

If the verb 'to be' is used with –ing form of a verb, verb 'to be' is cancelled.

They caught him. He was hiding under the table.

They caught him hiding under the table.

Exercise

Re write the following sentences according to the given clues :

1. Even though he is miserable, he keeps smiling. [in spite of the fact that]
2. The patient was given the best treatment yet he didn't survive. [despite]
3. David passed the interview even so he wasn't given the job. [though with yet]
4. In spite of the fact that he is handicap, he tackles critical situations wisely. [although]
5. Although the audience grew impatient, the orator kept speaking.[even though]
6. Though our complaints were acknowledged, the authorities didn't redress the complaints. [though]
7. Despite the fact that there are many shady trees. We can't camp here. [despite there]
8. There are many errors in your essay yet you got much better marks. [despite there]
9. He can follow the route though he is blind. [in spite of his]
10. The spectators didn't applaud even though the players made an amazing goal. [yet]

11. Although I am ready to accompany her, she doesn't want to go. [though with Yet]
12. Even though there is so much dust on the furniture, nobody wants to clean it. [in spite of there]

Adverb Clauses of Condition or Supposition

Conjunctions required are if, unless, provided that, supposing that, on condition that, as long as [the word that can be used or omitted]

Note : These clauses can be divided into three structures of verb agreement with different meanings.

A. These conditions don't guarantee a hundred percent assurance of the result.

Structure :

If + simple present or present continuous or present perfect or present perfect continuous goes with will or shall or may or can or should or must or simple present tense.

Example :

If he is studying hard, he will succeed.

Exercise :

Fill in the blanks with correct form of the given verbs according to the structures given above.

1. He----------(to be questioned) if he is involved.
2. If sushma---------------(ask) for help we won't deny it.
3. If students-----------------(not understand) the topic the teacher will explain it again.
4. Sangeeta will accompany you if you---------------(go) shopping.

CLAUSES

5. The lawn will look much better if they-------------(keep) it neat.
6. kavita will drop in if she-----------(have) time.
7. If Raghav------------(go) through these notes, he will secure good marks.
8. Asha will catch up with her friends if she----------- (run) faster.
9. If you have had your share, I----------------- (not/go/give) it to you again.
10. If she------------------(keep on sleep) she will get late to school.

B. Permanent Truth
Structure :

If + simple present tense, simple present tense

Example :

If water is heated to 100 degree centigrade, it boils.

Exercise:

Fill in the blanks with the given verbs In their correct tense.

1. If you pour oil on water, the oil ------- [float].
2. Curry ------ [become] watery if you -------- [add] more water into it than required.
3. If we ------- [not eat] for many days, our body ------ [get] weak.
4. If too spicy food ------- [eat], the digestive system -------- [damage].
5. The throat ------- [affect] if boiling tea ------ [gulp] down.

C. Unreal Conditions [imaginary]

Structure :

If + simple past, would + infinitive

Example :

If I were a bird, I would fly like a bird.

Exercise :

1. If she ------ [be] a grass hopper, her food ------- [be] leaves.
2. The king ------- [follow] your command if he ------ [be] your servant.
3. I ----- [do] much more work if I ------ [have] ten hands.
4. If he ------- [be] a tortoise, he ------- [not walk] as fast as a rabbit does.
5. She -------- [fly] all over the sky if she -------- [wear] those magic wings.

D. These conditions were real in life but they didn't happen.

Structure :

If + simple past tense, would + infinitive

If it rained, I would take out my umbrella.

Meaning :

It didn't rain so I didn't take out my umbrella.

Fill in the blanks with the given verbs in their past form according to the given structures.

1. If Suneeta -------- [meet] you last week, she ------- [tell] me.

    Answer : If Suneeta met you last week, she would tell me.

2. She ------- [pass] if she ------ [take] her studies seriously.
3. I -------- [wait] for you if you ------ [tell] me to do so.
4. If John -------- [receive] the notice, he -------- [tell] us.
5. Namrata -------- [telephone] me if she -------- [give] the message.
6. These houses -------- [demolish] if they -------- [be]under their plan.
7. If the driver ------- [take] the other route, we ------ [reach] home earlier.
8. Mary -------- [solve] this sum if she ------ [attempt] it.
9. Our maths teacher ------- [not present] if she ------- [not feel] well.
10. If the doctor --------- [diagnose] the disease properly, he ------ [prescribe] proper medicine.
11. The family -------- [not go] to the river side for picnic if they -------[know] the river would get so disastrously flooded.
12. If shops -------[open], we ------- [go] shopping.
13. I ------- [lend] him more money if I ------- [not buy] that camera.
14. If the party ------- [start] on time, we ----- [not be] so late.
15. If your friend ------ [find] guilty, he ------ [punish].

E. Structure :

If + past perfect, would + have + past participle

Note : Instead of 'would' other verbs could, might can also be used as suitable.

Example :

If he had had extra time, he would have helped you with your lessons.

Exercise :

Fill in the blanks with correct tense form of the given verbs according to the structure given above :

1. If I -----[have] the book, I -----[lend] it to you.

    Answer : If I had had the book, I would have lent it to you.

2. Mr. Goel ----- [get] wet if he ------- [not stand] under the shed.
3. George ------ [not advise] me if he ------ [not be] in my favour.
4. If it ------- [not be] for his abusive language, Father ----- [not beat] him.
5. The labourer ------- [do] extra work if the master ------ [agree] to pay him more.
6. If Ajali ------ [wear] woolens, she ------ [not catch] cold.
7. The scenery ------ [look] more attractive if it ----- [paint] in brighter colours.
8. The farmer ----- [not grumble] if his son ----- [help] in the field.
9. If I ------ [meet] you, I ------ [extend] you the invitation.
10. The campus ------ [not look] untidy if they ---- [not strew] the litter.
11. If they ------ [use] water carefully, there ----- [not be] such a great shortage.
12. The shopkeeper ------ [cheat] if he ----- [not be] vigilant.
13. If the beggar ----- [not misbehave], I ----- [give] him more money.
14. Mother ----- [be] very angry if Sonali ----- [tear] her dress.
15. If Renu ------ [have] her dinner, she ---- [tell] me.---

Conditional Clauses with Modal Verbs

A. Structures :

If + simple present, present perfect, present continuous, + should + infinitive;

Ought to + infinitive; must + infinitive; are to + infinitive; need + infinitive; may + infinitive; can + infinitive; will be able to + infinitive

Example :

If he has hidden your book, you should find it.

Exercise :

Complete the following sentences using correct form of the given verbs according to the given structures :

1. He ----- [not need] to rush if there ------ [be] still an hour to reach the station.

   Answer : He doesn't need to rush if there is still an hour to reach the station.

2. John ----- [take] care if you------ [inform] him about the danger he is in.

3. If they ----- [coming] by plane, they ----- [reach] here on time.

4. Students ------- [to inform] their parents if school timings ------ [changed].

5. If she ----- [attended] the meeting, she ------- [pass] on the message to the parents.

6. If Ramesh ------ [meet] with the accident, somebody ------ [contact] his relatives.

7. You ------ [consult] your elder brother if you ------ [not know] what to do.

8. If Jenny ------ [want] to appear for the interview, she ------ [prepare] herself.
9. Soldiers ------- [obey] the captain if he ------[command] the soldiers to do something.
10. If the tourists ------- [plan] to visit different sites, they ----- [hire] a bus.

B. Structure :

Modal verbs ought to, should and must show duty or obligation;must indicates

Stronger duty than others.

If + simple past, could + infinitive; would be able to + infinitive

If he bought that house, he could tell me.

Exercise:

Complete the following sentences according to the given structures :

1. If you didn't understand the sum, ------------------.
2. She would be able to submit the report on time if she ----------------.
3. These children wouldn't be so noisy if------------------.
4. Smith could accompany you if------------------.
5. If you requested Mr. Timothy, ------------------.
6. Bali would be able to jump over the fence if ------------------.
7. She might not lose her leg in that train accident if ---------.
8. If you came to school late, ------------------.
9. The house might be ransacked if------------------.
10. We could get in if --------------------.

C. Structure :

If + past perfect, might have + past participle; would + have + past participle;

Need + have + past participle

Exercise :

Re write the following sentences changing the verbs according to the given structures :

1. The teacher might advise you if she knew you were in trouble.

    Answer : The teacher might have advised you if you had been in trouble.

2. You didn't need to bargain if the quoted price was already so low.

3. I could get a helping hand if I asked for it.

4. If Raju broke the fence, he could tell his parents about it.

5. If people saw the injured man, they could take him to a nearby hospital.

6. You would be aware of the situation if you read the newspaper.

7. Students would leave the campus if there were chances of some trouble.

8. If she was given a proper role, she would happily take part in the drama.

9. All the participants would stay back if they were asked to do so.

10. The meeting could be short if they didn't argue unnecessarily.

Exercise :

Answer the given questions in complete sentences using the tense given in the question :

1. What will the students do if the teacher is absent?
2. What will happen if the doctor is out of station?
3. What would happen if the patient lost much blood?
4. What would the woman do if her chain was snatched?
5. What happens when milk boils over?
6. What might have happened if he had become bankrupt?
7. What will she do if her clothes are torn?
8. What could have happened if he had fallen from the tree top?
9. What would he do if he was slapped on his cheek?
10. What will happen if an accident takes place?
11. How would they study if the electricity went off?
12. What action should the girls have taken if they were eve – teased?

Exercise :

Re write the following sentences replacing the words possible, necessary, duty, probable and should in their correct tense form; make some other changes as well and 'Possible' can be replaced by 'can or could' 'necessary' can be replaced by 'need'. 'Probable' can be replaced by 'may or might '. 'Duty' can be replaced by 'must, ought to, or should '. Use 'must' for strong duty or obligation.

Exercise :

Give the meaning of each sentence :

1. The crop would have been harvested earlier if there had been bright sun shine.

   Meaning : The crop was harvested late because there wasn't bright sun shine.
2. One more room could be added if the land lord had sufficient funds.
3. There would be power shortage if the power station was damaged.
4. If he came to office, he would come to know about the changes in the policy.
5. If I were a bird, I would fly.
6. If he didn't work with dedication, he wouldn't be promoted.
7. If he had convinced the audience, he would have gotten full support.
8. My friend would leave this job if he found a better opportunity.
9. If he hadn't been cautious and hard working, he wouldn't have been a successful administrator.
10. His father would come to school immediately if he was informed about the accident he met with.
11. He would have been jailed if he had embezzled the money.
12. I f there hadn't been an extra bed in the hospital, the patient wouldn't have been admitted in the hospital.

Connector UNLESS in Conditional Clauses

Unless clause takes affirmative of a verb; 'If not 'can be replaced by 'unless '.

Exercise :

Rewrite the following sentences using unless :

1. If you don't take this route, you will reach home late.

   Answer : Unless you take this route, you will reach home late.

2. Father wouldn't get angry if you didn't break the window.

3. If we hadn't reached there on time, we wouldn't have had the opportunity to see the President of our country.

4. If we don't mow the lawn, the surroundings will look uncared for.

5. John won't accompany you if you don't ask him to do so.

6. If this shop doesn't have branded garments, the sale will reduce.

7. If you don't keep yourself warm, you'll get sick.

8. Driving on this road will remain risky if they don't repair it

9. Sudha will strain her eyes if she doesn't read in proper light.

10. Your legs will pain if you don't stop and take a rest.

Exercise :

Replace 'if not 'with 'unless 'and 'unless 'with 'if not ':

1. I won't be able to come to office on time unless I take a taxi.

2. He won't get the clearance unless he submits all the papers.

3. The sewing machine will not work smoothly if you don't get it repaired.

CLAUSES

4. We won't get seats to go to Goa if we don't get the booking done now.
5. You family will miss the cake ceremony if they don't reach here on time.
6. You won't be able to cope with this work if you don't eat well and take proper rest.
7. If you don't use your umbrella in this heat, your skin will be tanned.
8. You can buy this beautiful dress for the party unless you have got one already.

Note : The connector 'if 'can be replaced by provided that, supposing that, on condition that, as long as, in case. The word 'that' can be omitted.

Exercise :

Rewrite the following sentences replacing if with the given connectors :

1. Harry will buy this horse if it can be tamed.

   Answer : harry will buy this horse provided [that] it can be tamed.

2. If you don't reach by 12 : 30, I will leave home.
3. Kumars will go to Calcutta if you don't intend to spend your holidays with them.
4. If you are confident, they can't confuse you easily.
5. The programme will start on time if the chief guest isn't latte.
6. If your stomach is upset, don't eat this stuff.
7. Madhuri can dance much better if she practices more.
8. If my parents are able to afford, I will go for further studies.

Practice exercises A

Give all possible answers :

1. He never ---------unless you -------- him. [help, ask]
2. We -----------unless you --------- [be late, hurry up]
3. What if he -------too late?. [arrive]
4. What ---------we do if we --------- the bus?
5. If they ----------their assignment, they ------- trouble.
6. If I ---------promotion, I ----------a grand party.
7. Nothing -------- [do] unless someone ---------- [complain, complaint]
8. What ---------- happen if we miss the train?
9. They would be very popular if they ---------- according to the manifesto. (work)
10. The flight ------------[delay] if there ----------- fog.
11. If you ---------- her, ----------- her my regards.
12. You -----------the winner if you keep playing cautiously.
13. If I insisted, I ------------my money back.
14. If then naughty children ------------ my garden, I ----------- disheartened.
15. If you ---------- [lose] your temper, you ------------ in a mess,
16. If the curtains mismatched the paint, the house------------- [look] shabby.

Reported Speech
Direct and Indirect Speech

Rules to change direct speech into indirect speech (Reported Speech).

Reporting verb

REPORTED SPEECH

She **says**, "I am busy now."

will say

has said

is saying

When any of the underlined reporting verb is used, the verb in enclosed part doesn't change its tense. According to the situation the adverbs too may not change but the pronoun will change in the Indirect form of the sentence given above.

She says, "she is busy now."

Because pronoun 'I' refers to subject 'she', 'I' will change into subject pronoun 'she'.

Note : Direct Speech - He says to me, "I was wrong."

Indirect Speech – He tells me he was wrong.

Direct speech – You say to me, "I was wrong."

Indirect speech – You tell me I was wrong.

Because the subject is pronoun 'you' and 'I' is placed after the verb tell, 'I' refers to 'you'. So it changes into 'I'.

This change is because the subject of the reporting verb is 'you'.

If the reporting verb is say or said, they remain the same in the indirect speech as :

Direct - They say, "We are busy."

Indirect – They say they are busy.

Direct – They said, "We are busy."

Indirect – They said that they were busy."

If the reporting verbs is said to him change it into told him. ü Told to him.

Direct – Father said to Rohan, "They were in trouble."

Indirect – Father told Rohan that they were/had been in trouble.

Changes that take place in the indirect speech when reporting verb is 'said'.

A. Tense Changes

Present continuous like is playing – Change into past continuous – was playing

Present perfect – has done – had done

Simple past – wrote – had written, sometimes it remains the same 'wrote'

Simple future – will go – past future – would go

Shall go – should go

Can – could

May – might

Was – had been or was

Must – had to

Could – could have + past participle

Would – would have + past participle

Might – might have + past participle

Should – should have + past participle.

B. Now changes into then

This – that

These – those

Here – there

Ago – before

Just – then

C. Today – that day

to night – that night

tomorrow – the next day or the following day

yesterday – the previous day or the day before

last night – the night before or the previous night

next week – the following week.

D. Pronouns in the first person like, I, we, us, our, me and second person you' change into third person according to the situation. Second person you in direct speech is changed into the noun or pronoun coming after the reporting verb.

As : He say to me, "You are tired."

     He tells me that I am tired.

Third person like he, she, they remain unchanged.

As : He says to me, "He is tired."

     He tells me that he is tired.

If the reporting verb is made immediately or on the same spot, now, here, this, these, etc. are not changed. If the reported speech expressed universal truth or habitual fact, the tense is not changed.

As : The man said, "God is everywhere."

Indirect : The man said God is everywhere.

Direct – He said, "The evil that men do lives after them."

Indirect – He said that the evil that men do lives after them.

Kind of Sentences
Assertive Sentences
Exercise :

Change the following sentences into indirect speech. See the examples.

1. He said to me, "Your father has sent you a gift."

    Answer : He told me my father had sent me a gift.

2. Rajan said to us, "I cannot read if you make so much noise.

   Answer : Rajan told us he could not read if we made so much noise.

3. Aman said, "I am working against heavy odds."
4. Tom said, "I left school long ago."
5. Mohini said, "I do not know when the school is going to close for the vacations."
6. You said to me, "I am feeling very uneasy and tired. I would like to go to some hill-station.
7. The doctor said to me, "If you take this medicine regularly, you will soon get well."
8. He said to me, "Your teacher will be pleased with your work."
9. The boy said to his father, "Our examination is over."
10. My father said, "Virtue triumphs over evil."
11. You said to me, "You're wrong in your method."
12. Those elders said, "God is the Almighty Power."
13. The director said to the employee, "You may go now. I will see what can be done in this matter."
14. Thomas said, "No one can tell a man's character from his face."
15. He said, "The cow died last week."
16. Mr. Das said in front of three staff members. "I shall agree with what you propose if you sign this document."
17. Arun said, "Our brother arrived yesterday, but will go tomorrow."
18. The captain said, "These men will be on duty tonight."
19. My friend wrote to me, " I am unable to send you more than Rs. 500 but when I have more to spare, I will send you more."
20. Renuka said, "I am too busy to visit you this Saturday."

Interrogative Sentences
Group A
Rules to be followed in indirect speech.

1. Questions begin with an interrogative pronoun – what, who, which, whom and interrogative adverbs such as when, where, why, how, etc.

   The same interrogative pronouns and interrogative adverbs are used to begin these questions in in-direct speech.
2. The question is changed into assertive form.
3. The reporting verb is changed into ask, enquire etc.
4. The other rules which are followed while changing assertive sentences are the same for interrogative sentences.

Group B
Exercise
Change the following sentences into interrogative indirect speech.

Example :
(a) I said to him, "Who are you?"

Answer: Indirect – I asked him who he was.

1. Asha said to me, "Why do you not go home?"

   Answer : Asha asked me why I did not go home.
2. The master said to the servant, "Where do you come from?"
3. Mohan said to Sohan, "Why did you strike me?"
4. "Where are you going?" The teacher said to Rohan.
5. The teacher said to Rahel, "How does an elephant differ from other animals?"

6. The boss said to the secretary, "What do you mean by such behaviour?"
7. "Who are you, and what do you want here?" said the guard to the stranger.
8. "Where are the police?" said he.
9. The teacher said to the new comer, "What is your name? Where do you come from? Which school did you attend last?"
10. The Health Minister, Mathur said to the slum dwellers, "When did you get your children vaccinated?"
11. Mohan said to his father, "How were books written in ancient times? Who was the first person who found out how to print books? When did the first printing press come into the world?"
12. A student said to his teacher, "How does the Moon get its light? Why doesn't the Moon send out heat?"
13. The doctor said to the patient, "How many meals do you have a day?"
14. The wolf said to the lamb, "Why are you making the water muddy which I am drinking?"
15. A traveler said to some people in the crowd, "Why do all of you look sad? What is the matter?".
16. "What are you looking for?" said the first citizen to the second?" Have you lost anything?" said another, "Why do you carry a lighted lantern in broad day light?" shouted the third.
17. "What can I do for you?" the carpenter said to the customer.
18. The teacher said to the students, "What is a phrase?"
19. The boy said to his father, "Why can't this grass hopper be seen among green leaves?"
20. The guest said to the cook, "What spices did you use to prepare this delicious dish?"

REPORTED SPEECH

Interrogative Sentence : Which begin with verbs like is, are, am, was, were, has, have, do, does, will, shall, can, could, would, should, ought to, must etc.

Use 'if' or 'whether' to introduce the indirect speech. All other changes need to be done. Questions should be changed into statements.

A. Exercise

Change the following direct speech into indirect speech.

Example :

I said to Reeta, "Were you at school yesterday?"

Ans. I asked Reeta if or whether she had been / was at school the previous day?

1. "Have you anything to say on behalf of the accused?" said the judge to the counsel.
2. The teacher said to one of the students, "Can you tell me the cause of the Great war?"
3. "Have you any money to spare?" said Anand to his friend.
4. The mother said to her daughter, "Do you know where Sita is?"
5. "Did you feel better after taking this medicine?" the doctor said to the patient.
6. "Are you serious with your studies?" Father said to Sophia.
7. The volunteer said to the manager, "Am I needed when the function goes on?"
8. Ravi said to Rashmi, "Did you do it intentionally?"
9. The instructor said to his team, "Are you ready to bear this hardship?"

10. "Do you want pens or notebooks?" the stationer said to the customer.
11. "Are we gong to have a holiday tomorrow?" Neena said to her mother.
12. The passenger said at the counter. "Does the train stop at this platform?"
13. "Don't you sell lettuce?" the customer said to the green grocer.
14. "Is there a zoo in this locality?" Father said to the local people.
15. My friend said to me, "Did you reach the school on time?"
16. The incharge said, "Does this worker want to leave now?"
17. The guard said to the stranger, "Does this place look strange to you? Do you want me to helpyou?"
18. Mother said to Charles, "Have you enjoyed the meal?"
19. The old man said to the young boy, "Can you help me to cross the road?"
20. The visitor said to the waiter, "Can you clean the table before bringing my lunch?"

Imperative Sentences
Commands and Requests
Rules :

1. The reporting verb is changed into command, request or advice.

    Such as – request, order, tell, advice, beseech, threaten, beg, implore, command, ask, propose, forbid.

2. To _ infinitive is used

REPORTED SPEECH

3. Rules for changes are to be followed.
4. Generally 'that' is not used. If 'that' is used, instead of 'to' should is placed before the imperative

A. Exercises

Change the given direct speech into indirect speech.

Examples :

1. The invigilator said to the examinee, "Takeout all the chits of paper from your pockets."

   Answer Indirect speech

   The invigilator ordered the examinee to take out all the chits of paper from his pockets.

2. "Don't carry such a heavy bag, " Mother said to me.

   Indirect : Mother advised me not to carry such a heavy bag.

   1. Children said to their grand – mother, "Please tell us a story."
   2. Father said to his son, "Get out of my sight."
   3. The master said to the workers, "Work hard, you will get fruit of your labour."
   4. Raj said to me, "Lend me you pen, please."
   5. "Do not eat too many sweets, they will spoil your teeth, " The dentist said to the patient."
   6. Rohan said to Gopal, "Let us wait for our friends."
   7. The Co-ordinator said, "Let the boys go home."
   8. Mom said to us, "Let me work undisturbed."

      Note : When 'let' is used, use-propose, urge, suggest, that and should.
   9. He said to me, "Wait here till I return."

10. Father said to his son, "Put that book on the shelf when you have finished reading it."
11. Tanuj said, "Do not decide too hastily, Tanya."
12. The P.T. teacher said to the scouts, "Do not talk nonsense."
13. The girl said to her friend, "Please explain this sum to me."
14. Robin said to the boys, "Let us have a race and see who is the fastest runner."
15. "Away!" he said to the man, "and do not trouble your family any more."
16. Ivanhoe said to the servant, "Come early; I shall wait for you at the bridge.."
17. "Wake up my child, here is a friend waiting to see you," said the mother.
18. The lame man said, "Please give me your hand, I may fall down."
19. "Don't post the letter without showing it to me," my father said to me.
20. "Don't wait for me after nine O'clock", my father said to my mother, "I may eat out."

Exclamations and Wishes Exclamatory Sentences

Note : 1. Change the verb into – pray, cry, exclaim, wish, etc.
2. Omit interjections such as oh, bravo, hush, alas, hurrah, ah. Their sense may be indicated in the principal clause by means of an adverb or adverbial phrase.

Example

Direct : The child said, "Hurrah! Mother has come."

Indirect : The child exclaimed with delight that his mother had come.

REPORTED SPEECH

A. Exercise

I change the following exclamatory sentence into indirect speech.

1. The young boy said, "Alas ! we have lost the game." (exclaimed with sorrow)
2. 'Bravo, well done!' said the captain. (Exclaimed with excitement)
3. My uncle said, "May you live long !" (wish)
4. The child said, "Oh! It is my doll. (exclaimed happily)
5. "How glad I am, " said Thomas, "to meet my friend here." (use exclaimed happily)
6. This world", he declared, "is full of sorrow. Would that I were not born!" (exclaimed with sorrow and wished) use this help.
7. The emperor said, "Alas ! our foes are too strong."
8. William said, "Goodbye, my friends. May you live long!"
9. "Ah me!" said the captain, "What a rash and bloody deed you have done."
10. She said, "What a pity! You did not come."
11. "Long live the king !" echoed the audience.
12. "Hurrah!" cried the boy, " I have won the prize."

Change the given sentence into direct speech
Statements :

1. I told him that I had not seen them for months.
2. I told him that I would visit him the next day.
3. Mathur said that he had never liked that food.
4. Raj said that he was very tired and wanted to go to bed, .
5. John said that he wanted to be a soldier.

6. Abdul said that he had seen that movie and wouldn't watch it again.
7. The boy said that he would accompany them.
8. He said that the earth moves round the Sun.
9. Ravi told us that he had waited for them for two hours.
10. Rashmi said that she had come to meet them.
11. Maliny said though she had, come, it was against her will.
12. The speaker says that it gives him great pleasure to be here this evening.
13. The teacher told the class that the Equatorial region has very high temperature and much rain.
14. The host told the guests that he was happy as all of them accepted the invitation.

Interrogative Sentences

Change the following sentences into direct speech.

1. The child asked his father when the train would arrive.
2. Ravi asked me why Ramesh hadn't come to visit the Taj Mahal.
3. He asked me if I had any doubts.
4. Aman asked Ravi if he would change places with him.
5. The old mouse asked who would bell the cat.
6. He asked me what I wanted.
7. The stranger asked Alice where she lived.
8. He said to himself where his slippers were.
9. The lady inquired if he had fully recovered.
10. The leader of the group asked them whether they would listen to such a man.

11. The mother asked her son where he had been the whole day.
12. Reema asked Arjun if he had read that letter.
13. The king asked the wise man whom he thought the happiest man was living.

Imperative Sentences

Change the given indirect speech into direct speech.

1. He asked Ravi to go with him.
2. The boss ordered his employee to leave the room and told him not to return.
3. Father advised his sons not to quarrel among themselves when he was dead.
4. My mother told me to get in and sit down as she had to have a serious talk with him.
5. The speaker suggested to them to try to unite the two parties.
6. Alexander requested his father to let him ride on his horse.
7. The stranger to the farmer to bring him a glass of milk.
8. The captain ordered the boys to sitdown..
9. The railway guard advised the passengers not to be impatient. Each of them would get their seats according to their seat numbers, .
10. The interviewer advised the candidate not to read so fast.
11. The monitor ordered the students not to shout; otherwise he would call the Discipline Incharge.
12. Mother told my younger brother not to play outside.

Exclamatory Sentences

Change the given indirect speech into direct speech.

1. The man exclaimed excitedly that he had never seen such an animal.
2. The girl exclaimed sadly that she had lost her favourite doll in the river.
3. The spectators exclaimed happily that their country was winning the game.
4. The student who always ranked first in her class cried softly for having lost her rank.
5. Mannu shouted fearfully that he had a horrible dream that night.
6. The team leader exclaimed happily that his team was playing brilliantly.

Fill in the blanks according to the given dialogue.

1

Prince : You have fairly won the prize.

Michael : Thank you, your highness. It was because of your blessings.

Prince : I will double up your reward if you give your services to my kingdom.

Michael : Pardon me, noble Prince, but I have vowed to serve someone else.

The prince told Michael he (a) _____won the prize. Michael replied to his highness with thanks and said that it (b) _____ because of his blessings. The prince said that he (C) _____ double up (d) _____ reward if he _____. Services to his kingdom. Michael begged to pardon the noble prince but said (f) _____ _____ _____ to serve someone else.

REPORTED SPEECH

2

Villager : This place looks like a heaven.

Companion : Why do you think so?

Villager : Don't you see neat and tidy buildings?

Companion : Is it only the buildings which make the city heavenly?

Villager : Can't you see broad roads without any pits?

Companion : Oh ! yes this place is really heavenly. The greenery, the flowers, the water falls, trees, with fresh leaves add to its heavenly look.

The villager told his companion (a) _____ place (b) _____ like heaven. The companion asked the villager why (c) _____ (d) _____ so. The villager exclaimed with surprise (e) _____ he (f) _____ neat and tidy buildings. The companion replied if it (g) _____ only the buildings which (h) _____ the city heavenly. The village asked (i) _____ _____ _____ _____ without any pits. The companion exclaimed in agreement that (j) _____ place (k) _____ really heavenly. The greenery, the flowers, the water falls, trees (l) _____ fresh leaves (m) _____ to its heavenly look.

3

Doctor : Why did you not take medicines regularly?

Patient : I am sorry, doctor. I am very forgetful.

Doctor : If you are so forgetful, I can't treat you.

Patient : Please don't stop my treatment.

Doctor : How can I get you cured?

Patient : I will not forget to take my medicines regularly.

The doctor asked the patient why he (a) _____ (b) _____ regularly. The patient replied (c) _____ very forgetful. The doctor said if (d) _____ so forgetful (e) _____ _____ treat (f) _____. (h) _____ _____ treatment. The doctor said confusedly how (i) _____ _____ get(j) _____ cured. The patient said that (k) _____ _____ not forget to take (l) _____ medicines regularly.

4

Guest : Can you book a single room for me?

Incharge : Yes, sir ! I can.

Guest : What are the charges?

Incharge : Rs. 1000.

Guest : What will be the total charges with three meals?

Incharges : It will be 2500.

Guest : Ok book my room and show it to me.

The guest asked the Incharge (a) _____ _____ _____ a single room for him. The incharge told him that (b) _____ _____. The guest asked him for the charges. The Incharge told (c) _____ that it (d) _____ Rs. 1000. The guest asked him (e) _____ (f) _____ the with three meals. The Incharge told him that (g) _____. The guest agreed and told him (h) _____ (i) _____ and (j) _____.

5

Blind beggar : I want to cross the road.

Boy : OK, hold my hand.

Beggar : Please don't walk fast.

Boy : I know uncle. I will be careful.

Beggar : Son, you are very helpful.

The blind beggar told the boy that (a) _____ to cross the road. The boy agreed to do so and told him (b) _____ _____ hand. The beggar requested him (c) _____ fast. Calling the beggar uncle the boy replied that he (d) _____.. He (e) _____ _____ careful. The beggar called the boy son and told him, he was very helpful.

6

Mother : Don't bite you nails.

Son : Why are you telling me so?

Mother : Your teeth will become shapeless.

Son : I don't think so.

Mother : Nail biting will become your habit. You will btie them even when you have your children.

Mother advised her son (a) _____ his nails. The son asked (b) _____ telling, him so. Mother said that (c) _____ _____ become shapeless. The son replied that (d) _____ so. Mother warned him and told him that nail biting (e)_____ _____ his habit. Even when he (f) _____ _____ children.

Active and Passive Voice
Note :

1. Sentences which have transitive verbs, can be changed into passive voice.
2. Many times the passive voice sentence does not intend to high light the doer

   As :

   Active voice : Someone was throwing stones.

Passive voice : Stones were being thrown.

It is not necessary to mention 'someone' as it does not denote special person.

But

As :

Active voice : Mr. Das posted the letter

Passive voice : The letter was posted by Mr. Das.

The particular person – Mrs. Das posted the letter, so his name has to be mentioned.

3. Sentences which have intransitive verbs or link verbs (mentioned in chapter verbs) can't be changed into passive voice.

    Example : They **are working** carefully intransitive verb.

    It **feels like** a rug. Link verb.

4. Past participle is used in passive voice

    As: They grew vegetables. Active voice

    Vegetables were **grown** by them.

    Grown is past participle of 'grew'.

    'were' shows that the action was done in the past.

Follow the given table to change verbs in different tenses to make passive voice.

Active Voice	Passive Voice
Simple present	
Draw	is drawn, are drawn, am drawn
Cooks	is cooked, are cooked
Writes	is written, are written

ACTIVE AND PASSIVE VOICE

Active voice	**Passive voice**
Simple past	
Threw	was thrown, were thrown
Blew	was blown, were blown
Wrote	was written, were written

Active voice	**Passive voice**
Present continuous	
Is teaching	is being taught, are being taught
Are cooking	

Active Voice	**Passive Voice**
Was telling	was being told
Were telling	were being told

Active voice	**Passive Voice**
Present perfect	
Has done	has been done
Have saved	have been saved

Past Perfect	
Had given	had been given

Simple future	
Will, shall study	will be, shall be studied

Future Perfect	
Will have completed	will have been completed
Shall have made	shall have been made

Modal Verbs

Passive Voice
Can do - can be done
Could break – could be broken
Should punish – should be punished
Ought to complain – ought to be complained

Passive Voice
will study – will be studied
would read – would be read
may see – might be seen, may be seen
might understand – might have been understood

A. Exercise

Change the following sentences into passive voice

1. Children watch cartoon series.
   Answer : Cartoon series are watched by children.
2. My mother cooks delicious food.
   Answer : Delicious food is cooked by my mother.
3. Tourists visited Jim Corbet Park.
4. Rohit tore my important notes.
   Answer : Important notes were torn by Rohit.
5. I bought different vegetables.
6. Maths teacher helped him as he had some doubts.
7. A herd of elephants broke the fence.
8. You can take this chair.
9. Anu has joined coaching classes.
10. Dogs are snatching the poor man's food.
11. The school rules do not allow students to come to school without Identity cards.
12. The fish will die if people throw garbage into the river.

ACTIVE AND PASSIVE VOICE

13. Citizens ought not to disobey law and order.
14. The shopkeeper does not give discount on any thing.

    Answer : Discount isn't given on any thing by the shopkeeper.
15. The archaeologists couldn't find the possessions of the dead king.
16. Some people felled the trees.
17. The players have played the game brilliantly.

    Answer : The game has been played brilliantly.
18. They have sold out oil so the people are suffering.
19. Did the mob destroy shops?

    Answer : Shops were destroyed by the mob.
20. Didn't they know the way to station?
21. Does she make such beautiful dolls?
22. Can you write this application?
23. Will the parents take the sick boy to the doctor?
24. Has she copied these notes?
25. Students shouldn't throw wrappers in the lawn.
26. Shepherds are taking the cattle to the grazing ground.
27. Father might buy some burgers for us.
28. My mother gave me an expensive mobile.
29. I bought you some fruit.
30. The discipline incharge told the students not to make noise.
31. Dirty smog has polluted the air.
32. Today I am watching a film
33. I studied your proposal but I am sorry I can't accept it.
34. You have already given the complaint.

35. Mr. Kumar saw the Blue Nile Falls several years ago.
36. The Lals have eaten Ethiopian food.
37. The Ethiopians speak Amharic
38. Teachers from different countries taught different subjects in the school where the writer also taught.
39. I saw this gentleman somewhere.

B. Exercise

Note : Transitive verbs with prepositions, imperative verbs and in complex sentences

Change the following sentences into passive voice.

1. He listened to me.

   Answer : I was listened to.

2. Did he stare at you?

   Answer : You weren't stared at.

3. He will object to my proposal.
4. Do it at once. (use let)
5. Write a letter to your brother. (let and should can be used)
6. Do not beat the dog. (use 'should')

   Answer : The dog should not be beaten.

7. Carry it home. (let, should)
8. The director will notify the students that the Geography exam will be next Friday.
9. The teacher expected Solomon to secure A's in all the subjects.
10. Sahel must inform me if he has circulated the notice.
11. We have to tell them to distribute all the books among the students of class 10.

ACTIVE AND PASSIVE VOICE

12. Brother will advise her to go abroad for higher education.
13. While I was explaining the lesson, one student was busy with his mobile phone. (complex).
14. The Prime minister named the ship – "Sea Gull."
15. We left the room open.
16. The nurse found the patient restless.
17. They considered the plan foolish.
18. Father made her a table (VT4)
19. The wind blew off the candle. (preposition)
20. The banks pay interest on deposits.
21. Father is fixing my brother's bicycle.
22. The concerned people were shooting scenes for their film when I passed by.
23. Do robots paint pictures?
24. Put the pictures on those walls.
25. How much did you pay for this watch?
26. Farmers don't grow wheat in this region.
27. Have all the students paid the fees?
    Answer : Has fees been paid by all the students?
28. What does this factory produce?
29. Did they hire a taxi to go to Delhi?
    Answer : Was a taxi hired to go to Delhi?
30. We could send the parcel only by sea.

Noun Clause : Change into passive voice
Example :
People expected him to win the fight. Active voice

Passive voice :

    (a) He was expected to have won the fight.

    (b) It was expected from him to win the fight.

Change only the main clause into passive voice.

Exercise :

1. They notified us when to expect the guests.
2. You should remind me to leave early.
3. You will never persuade him to follow their advice.
4. Neeta always tells her friend to be neat and clean.
5. We are informing you not to take the next train.
6. The Head is notifying the committee to study the case earnestly.
7. The elders shall persuade Renu Madan to take genuine steps.
8. You can tell your mother to expect the guests this evening.

Direct and Indirect Object (their places change in passive voice)

Note :

The direct and indirect objects

Example :

Robert made him a wire bicycle.

Direct object – a wire bicycle.

Indirect object – him

    Change their places using the preposition 'for' answer : Robert made a wire bicycle for him

ACTIVE AND PASSIVE VOICE

Passive voice :

A wire bicycle was made for him by Robert.

Exercise

Change the places of direct and indirect objects making active voice sentence and then change them into passive voice as the examples given above.

    A. While changing the places of objects you may use 'to' when following verbs are used. Paid, lend, gave, read, throw, tell, handed, wished, deny, etc. brought, show

    B. Use 'for' when following verbs are used. Made, bought, leave, ordered, do, spare, get etc.

Note : Follow the directions given under the exercise

1. The customer gave the shopkeeper Rupees 2000.
2. She bought her son liner skates.
3. The magician showed us numerous tricks.
4. Please don't throw us the ball.
5. A gentleman has left you a message.
6. He brought them some cookies.
7. The office bearer handed me some files.
8. Uncle wished us happy Christmas.
9. Please do me a favour.
10. Can you spare him a pair of shoes.
11. The shopkeeper brought us some rare fruits.
12. The customer paid the cashier the bill.
13. You can't deny the customers this offer.
14. Please tell me the secret.
15. My friend lent me the book just for one day.

Exercise :

Change the following sentence into active voice

Mixed Forms

1. He was laughed at by all his friends.

    Answer : All his friends laughed at him.

2. All the children were given a piece of advice by their grand-father.

    Answer : Their grand-father gave all the children a piece of advice.

3. The teacher was pleased with the boy's work.
4. Why should I not be taken into your confidence?
5. Am I mistaken for a doctor?
6. He was seen opening the door.
7. Raman was heard to call out your name.
8. She has been made to complete the homework.
9. Let the order be given.
10. Promises should be kept.
11. I was struck by his unique appearance.
12. The plan has been approved by the sub-committee.
13. I have been given much cause for anxiety.
14. The student was granted permission by the teacher.
15. Have my orders been carried out by you?
16. The story was listened to eagerly.
17. The injured victims were carried to hospital by the rescuers.
18. The tree was uprooted by the storm.
19. We were greatly delighted by the singing of the birds.
20. This new watch was given to me by my husband.
21. Not a drum was heard.

ACTIVE AND PASSIVE VOICE

22. By whom was this speech given?
23. Our lives are spent in expectations.
24. Do not be daunted by challenges?
25. Have not many been ruined by gambling?

Edit the following sentences

In each line one word is wrong write wrong word on the left and the correct word on its right.

1

Yesterday when football is being played	(a)	_____	_____
a player fall down because he was	(b)	_____	_____
hitted by another. The game was	(c)	_____	_____
stop and the injured player was	(d)	_____	_____
took away from the field to	(e)	_____	_____
be give first aid.	(f)	_____	_____

2

First the disease will be diagnose.	(a)	_____	_____
Then some tests like urine, blood etc,	(b)	_____	_____
have to be take. When the doctor	(c)	_____	_____
Understand what the disease is,	(d)	_____	_____
he will started treating the	(e)	_____	_____
Patient. People go to doctor when	(f)	_____	_____
there disease becomes complicated	(g)	_____	_____

3

The child received a beautiful	(a) _____ _____
Toy car. He always sleep	(b) _____ _____
With it. One day when he come	(c) _____ _____
from school, he find the	(d) _____ _____
breaked car. He started	(e) _____ _____
to cried. His mother	(f) _____ _____
hug him and the child slept	(g) _____ _____

4

A tortoise is cover with a	(a) _____ _____
hard shell which protect	(b) _____ _____
Its soft body from get	(c) _____ _____
injure. It walks so slowly	(d) _____ _____
that it can't took race against	(e) _____ _____
any animal but once it participate	(f) _____ _____
in a race with a hare. To	(g) _____ _____
the reader's surprised the tortoise	(h) _____ _____
defeat the hare.	(i) _____ _____

One word is missing, write it correctly, and also two words between which it is.

1

When the tree has cut down,	(a) _____ _____ _____
The woodcutter will taking	(b) _____ _____ _____
Its logs home. The wood has be	(c) _____ _____ _____

ACTIVE AND PASSIVE VOICE

Used a building material. (d) _____
He has planned (e) _____
Construct beautiful (f) _____
house.

2

The road jam packed last (a) _____
Monday.
The vehicles on standstill. (b) _____
I had reach the office (c) _____
time but the traffic would (d) _____
move slowly. you believe (e) _____
how hours I was stuck (f) _____
up.

3

Floods destroy lives (a) _____
property. Houses have (b) _____
swept
away like toys. How can (c) _____
this loss
recovered? How can the (d) _____
dead
alive? Cloud bursts can't (e) _____
stopped.
Fear the Lord ! our lives (f) _____
in His hands

CONJUNCTIONS

Conjunctions are of different types-
1) Co-ordinating
2) Co-relating
3) Subordinating

Co-ordinating conjunctions

They join noun + noun – the boy and the girl, dog and cat, shirts and pants, paper and pencil, bat and ball, butter and milk, Sudha and Suhani, bed and chair, Delhi and Mumbai.

Anger and joy, happiness and sorrow, sweetness and bitterness, bravery and cowardly, smartness and shabbiness, clumsiness and laziness.

Note - The nouns in first group are common and proper nouns. Second group are absract nouns.

The following exercises can take 'and' + nouns.

1) The school officials bought some _____, _____ for school children.
2) Raju came to this shop to buy _____ _____ milk.
3) This new mall sells branded _____ _____ pants. Many people like to buy them from there.
4) There is a strange sound outside _____ _____ cats must be fighting.
5) _____ _____ _____ are needed to write.

CONJUNCTIONS

A. Exercise

Fill in the blanks connecting two nouns, adverbs and adjectives, verbs.

1) _____ and _____ affect one's health, one has deteriorating effect and the other has positive effect.
2) The way we _____ and _____ ourselves reflect our _____ and _____.
3) The courage of a soldier results into his _____ or _____.
4) Gourd and _____ of Papaya have their own beneficial effects on our health.
5) He likes to sleep most of the time and doesn't work. This causes _____ and _____ which result into his poverty.

Note- The word 'and' can join two adjectives, two adverbs, two phrases, two clauses (main clause) and verbs.

B. Exercise

Change the clues into their correct form.

1) Talking _____ (angry) or _____ (rude) spoils one's reputation. (use adverb)
2) It's up to you. You can go _____ the hill or _____. Go down the hill, climb up (phrases)
3) The road goes _____, or _____ (along the river, through the forest) (phrases)
4) Some people keep their houses _____ or dirty; it depends upon their own mood. (adjectives)
5) This letter is brief _____. (Or complete, but complete)
6) The road is smooth _____. A) But quite long, b) or quite long
7) The child was _____. A) tired but didn't want to stop playing b) tired but wanted to sleep.

8) Samyak worked hard _____. A) and didn't fruit of his labour B) but he didn't get fruit of his labour.

9) The guests can play with us _____. A) or they can stay with their relatives. B) and we will give all the comfort.

10) People don't like to walk on muddy fields _____. A) and children like to play their b) but children like to play there.

11) My sister will like this dress with beautiful embroidery _____. A) but she will not like that dress with so many frills. B) or she will not like that dress with so many frills.

12) The driver may have taken the longer route. A) or the shorter route b) and shorter route

13) The customer may buy all the mangoes _____ because he seems to be more interested in mangoes. A) or he may buy all the oranges b) but he may not buy all the oranges.

14) She has to reach the airport on time; _____ (or else, but) miss the flight.

15) Some bottles are filled with water _____ (but, if) some bottles are empty.

Co-Relative Conjunctions

Some conjunctions work in pairs.

As well as, both _ and, though_ yet, not only_ but also, either_ or, neither_ nor, whether_ or, so_ that, enough to, too.

A. Exercise

Fill in the blanks using conjunctions given above.

1) The teachers _____ the students are enjoying the trip.

2) _____ my father _____ yours are going to visit the site. They want to build their houses.

3) None of us knows _____ they will settle in the USA _____ in Canada.

4) _____ the labourers at the construction site sweat out extensively, _____ they are paid the least.
5) The children are playing _____ well _____ they have 99% chances of winning the award.
6) Rohit is _____ patient _____ considerate. Many a times he gave up what he deserved.
7) This soup is _____ tasteless.
8) Sonya is intelligent _____ _____ solve the sums.
9) _____ the Principal _____ the director will address the guests.
10) _____ Sarita _____ Sonam won the competition.

Some Other Conjunctions

Hence, consequently, however, nevertheless, moreover, besides, nonetheless, otherwise, or else, despite, in spite of.

Note - Hence and consequently mean as a result. However, nevertheless, nonetheless mean there were difficulties but still the result was positive. Moreover, means along with one benefit another was also given.

A. Exercise

Fill in the blanks with appropriate connector.

1) The sheep were taken to a grassland; _____ they ate well. (then, hence, since)
2) Roy increased his business with hard work and tactfully; _____ ; he has established his business in many countries. (consequently, hence, both)
3) Doctor Das is an efficient doctor; _____ he is dedicated to his profession. (moreover, but, since)
4) Mr. Paul works continuously for hours; _____ no needy is turned back without a smile from his door step. (none the less, what so ever, hence)

5) Mr. Raj is sick; _____ he comes to office on time and works diligently. (besides, however, consequently)

6) There was no hope of his surviving; _____ he recovered fully. (never the less, hence, besides)

7) The manager said to one of the office workers; you had better give good results _____ you will be demoted. (moreover, also, or else)

8) _____ being advised, Rajat keeps on annoying other workers. (Despite of, Despite, In spite of)

9) _____ his wealth, he is very humble. (in spite, despite, though)

10) Leave the company of such people; _____ get ruined. (but, or else, since)

11) _____ the bore-hole is not covered, children play near it. (despite of the fact that, inspite of the fact that, in spite of the fact that)

12) The Government is paying for these children's uniform, books, tuition fees; _____ for mid-day meals yet their parents are reluctant to send them to school. (besides, neither, either)

13) _____ Renu is living in fresh air, clean environment, and eating healthy food, she is becoming weaker and weaker. (despite the fact that, in spite of the fact that, all)

14) Diving into that deep sea, demanded his fearlessness _____ he became well known all over the world. (hence, therefore, consequently, all)

15) Stop disturbing me; _____ I will push you. (otherwise, or else, all)

Subordinating Conjunctions
Subordinating conjunctions for different clauses.
Time clauses- when, while, after, before, till, until

CONJUNCTIONS

Reason clause- because, as, since, seeing that, now that, considering that

Adjective clause- who, whom, whose, which, where, that, h

Noun clause- who, whom, whose, which, where, that, how

Conditional clause- if, unless, provided (that)

Clauses of contrast or concession -Though, although, even though, though _ _ yet

Clauses of result- so _ _ that, such _ _ that,

Phrases- too _ _ to, enough _ _to

Example:

The soup is too salty to drink. The soup is warm enough to drink.

Purpose clause- so that, in order that

Phrases 1) to + non-finite - I am reading this book to enjoy it.
        2) so as + non-finite
        3) in order to – non-finite

Note- Look for the section where clauses are given.

Clauses of Comparison

As _ _ as, more _ _ than, than, as, as if, not more than, even more.

Note - use different degrees of comparison.

Formation of Comparitives

1. Add -r and -est after the adjective which end with a vowel.

Positive Degree	Comparative Degree	Superlative Degree
Large	Larger	largest
Fine	Finer	Finest

| Close | closer | Closest |
| Wide | wider | Widest |

2. By doubling the end consonant and adding -er and -est respectively to the adjective one syllabus ending in a consonant proceeded by a vowel.

Positive	**Comparitive**	**Superlative**
Fat	Fatter	Fattest
Thin	Thinner	Thinnest
Flat	Flatter	Flattest
Sad	Sadder	Saddest
big	Bigger	Biggest

3. By adding -er and -est respectively to the adjective of one syllable.

Positive	**Comparative**	**Superlative**
High	Higher	Highest
Quiet	Quieter	Quietest
Near	nearer	nearest
dear	Dearer	Dearest

4. Remove- 'y' and add – 'ier' and 'iest' to the adjectives which have two syllables.

Positive	**Comparative**	**Superlative**
Healthy	healthier	Healthiest
Wealthy	Wealthier	Wealthiest
Happy	Happier	Happiest
Noisy	Noisier	Noisiest
Heavy	Heavier	Heaviest

Note- syllable means sounds the vowels make.

CONJUNCTIONS

5. Put 'more' or 'most' when an adjective has two or more syllables.

Positive	Coparative	Superlative
Intelligent	More intelligent	Most intelligent
Beautiful	More beautiful	Most beautiful
Ignorant	More ignorant	Most ignorant
Careless	More careless	Most careless
Industrious	More industrious	Most industrious

6. Irregular Comparitives and Superlatives

Positive	Comparative	Superlative
Little	less	Least
Good	Better	Best
Bad	Worse	Worst
far	Farther, further	Farthest
much	More	Most
old	Older, elder	Oldest, eldest

A. Exercise

Fill in the blanks using degrees of comparison or superlative degree.

1) Sohan is _____ (brave) than Siddharth. Ans- braver
2) Sharu is the _____ (healthy) man among all these wrestlers. Ans- healthiest
3) The red rose is _____ (beautiful) than the white rose.
4) The monitor is _____ (tall) boy in their class.
5) Renu is _____ intelligent _____ her sister.
6) Nidhi is _____ (pretty) _____ her friend.
7) Your younger brother looks _____ (big) _____ you.

8) Kamala is _____ _____ (smart) girl in this group.
9) This is _____ _____ (broad) road I have ever seen.
10) Sulekha's work is _____ than (neat) Rahel's work.
11) The _____ (fast) runner among these boys is Deepak.
12) The white horse is _____ attractive _____ the brown horse.
13) My dog is _____ (stronger) _____ Harry's dog.
14) Mr. Thomas has contributed _____ _____ for the Annual function of the orphanage.
15) Iron is _____ useful _____ any other metal.
16) I have read many chapters from the book. The _____ (last, form, former) ones are _____ interesting than the latter ones.
17) The last chapters of the story are _____ thrilling than the previous ones.
18) The majority accepted the _____ proposal. (late, latter)
19) We expect to get the _____ (late, latest) news in a few minutes.
20) This year's function is _____ (good, better) than that of last year.
21) Chandigarh is not _____ cool in Manali. (such cool, as/ so cool, as)
22) The seat you are sitting on is _____ (hard) than my seat. (hard, harder, hardest)
23) This task isn't _____ easy _____ you think. (such as, so, as)
24) The competition I sat for was _____ (tough) _____ I though.

CONJUNCTIONS

Mixed Connectors (Conjunctions)
Exercise :
Fill in the blanks using conjunctions.
1. That student is lazy _____ intelligent.
2. It doesn't make any difference _____ long _____ you are honest.
3. _____ your ill health, you continued to do your duties.
4. The guilty man will be punished _____ _____ he falls down on his knees.
5. They are looking forward to put this house on rent _____ they have bought a bigger house.
6. These vegetables are fresh _____ we will buy some.
7. _____ Raju _____ Anil have settled abroad.
8. The yellow building is _____ high _____ the white building.
9. Their parents have agreed to take them on a picnic _____ they do their exams well.
10. _____ Nainital _____ also Shimla are covered with snow.
11. _____ your English and Geography book are with me.
12. _____ it was raining, the children played in-door games.
13. I will wait here _____ you return.
14. The guests have gone to visit their friends _____ to see some historical monuments.
15. Do you know the girl _____ gave me this book?
16. I know my neighbours _____ they came to this house in 1989.
17. _____ a person grows, he should become mature.

18. I don't know _____ he had come from.
19. Can you clear my doubts _____ you have completed your work?
20. _____ I knew you would visit us, I would stay at home.
21. _____ our car has run out of fuel, it can not take us any further.
22. They broke their friendship went apart.
23. I was annoyed _____ I kept quiet.
24. We visited our friends _____ relatives.
25. Ravi ran _____ fast _____ get the award.
26. Human beings should be _____ social and diligent _____ ants.
27. Mother said to her daughter, "You can choose _____ this dress _____ that
28. _____ house hold duties a school Principal has to monitor the management of her school.
29. Mr. Kumar is prompt _____ carries out his duties efficiently.
30. _____ _____ I am busy, I will give some time to you later.
31. He is all right _____ quite fatigued.
32. Though he is poor _____ he looks cheerful.
33. She proved herself innocent _____ she was forgiven.
34. You have to sit in the class quietly _____ get out.
35. God wants human beings to live happily _____ enjoy His wondrous creation.
36. That boy is _____ kind _____ he gives away his lunch to the boy who doesn't have any food to eat.

CONJUNCTIONS

37. The orator gave such a long speech _____ the audience started feeling sleepy.
38. The old man is not only hungry _____ also thirsty.
39. Mr. Das _____ his wife can attend the meeting.
40. Ranjeet didn't learn his dialogue well _____ he was confused.
41. Take this seat _____ that one.
42. My friends _____ yours enjoyed the game.
43. Walk noiselessly _____ let the birds fly away.
44. I reached the air – port on time _____ you didn't
45. Don't throw the garbage here and there; _____, it will create unhygienic conditions all around.

ADVERB

An Adverb is a word which modifies a verb, an adjective or an adverb.

How are the underlined words working?
1) All these boys play <u>brilliantly</u>.
   Manner adverb.
2) He is a <u>very smart</u> boy.
   'smart' adjective modifying the noun 'boy'. 'Very' adverb modifying the adjective 'smart'.
3) The chances of her getting selected in the interview are much more remote.
   'Remote' is an adjective modifying the noun 'chances'.
   'much' is an adverb modifying the adverb 'more'.
   'more' is an adverb modifying the adjective 'remote'.

Classification of Adverbs
Adverb of Manner- Reena sings melodiously.

A. Exercise

beautifully, brightly, intelligently, ferociously, attractively, cunningly, beautifully, swiftly, quickly, neatly, bravely, perfectly, calmly, quietly Sadly,

ADVERB

Answer the following questions using adverb of manner.

1) How did the soldiers fight?
   (Ans) The soldiers fought <u>bravely</u>.
2) How do elephants attack?
3) How should we keep our pets?
4) How did your friend react when she got the news of her sister's demise?
5) How did the chief detective plan out the search of the criminal?
6) How does she dress up when she goes to parties?
7) How do the snakes slither out of sight?
8) How was the scenic beauty presented?
9) How did the fox take away the cheese from the crow?
10) How did he do his exams?

Manner Adverbs have positive, comparative and superlative degrees.

Positive Degree	Comparative Degree	Superlative Degree
Beautifully	More Beautifully	Most Beautifully
Wise	More Wisely	Most Wisely
Early	Earlier	Earliest
Sadly	More Sadly	Mostly Sadly
Swiftly	More Swiftly	Most Swiftly
Skilfully	More Skilfully	Most Skilfully

Adverb of one syllable take-r in comparative degree and -est in the superlative degree.

Positive Degree	Comparative Degree	Superlative Degree
Fast	Faster	Fastest

| Long | Longer | Longest |
| Hard | Harder | Hardest |

Irregular Comparative Degree and Superlative Degree

Positive Degree	Comparative Degree	Superlative Degree
Ill, Badly	Worse	Worst
Well	Better	Best
Much	More	Most
Little	Less	Least
Near	Nearer	Nearest
Fast	Farther/Further	Farthest/Furthest

A. Exercise

Fill in the blanks with the correct degree of the given adverb.

1) Taruna runs _____ than her sister. (fast, faster, more faster)

2) The second candidate answered the question _____ than the third. (confident, more confidently, most confidently)

3) Steal chairs are _____ (strong) than the wooden chairs.

4) Solomon was the _____ (earlier, earliest) to arrive.

5) It was the _____ party I had ever attended. (bad, worse, worst)

6) Our houses are far from the railway station, but yours is the _____ (near, nearer, nearest)

7) The labourer cried _____ (bitter) as his friend died under wreckage.

8) To earn living one must work _____ (hardly, hard)

ADVERB

9) Sudha sings _____ than Ratna. (sweet, more sweetly, sweetly)
10) Even the _____ student of our class submitted the assignment on time. (lazy, lazier, laziest)

Adverb of Time

> Yesterday, today, tomorrow, recently, before, after, still, then, now, lately, soon, just now, yet, just then

B. Exercise

Fill in the blanks using adverbs of time given above.

1. Children are playing in the garden _____.
2. _____ they have played the game, they will take a bath.
3. Mr. Das said that he would leave for Delhi _____.
4. _____ the fishermen go fishing, they will collect nets.
5. They have _____ reached the station, the train will leave in a few minutes.
6. I won't buy the ticket for this film as I saw it _____.
7. I met those people _____.
8. Anjali told me that the group left for Nainital _____.
9. The guests will be arriving _____.
10. The principal called him to her office _____.
11. Father hasn't come home _____.
12. The boy has cut down the tree _____ _____; a stranger has come to help.

Adverbs of Frequency

These adverbs show how often an action occurs.

> Generally, always, often, regularly, never, every day, occasionally, seldom, twice a day, frequently, rarely, sometimes

Placing frequency verbs

a) Place it between subject – and one word verb.

Example: Rajan's mother always buys grocery from this shop.

b) If more than two verb forms are used, place the frequency adverb between the two verb forms.

Example: I have never disturbed the teacher.

c) If the verb is, are or am is used, the adverb is placed after the verb.

Example: the doctor is usually late.

A. Exercise

Arrange these words into sentences.

1) Go/students/hardly/school/my/picnic/from/on
2) Me/friends/childhood/never/my/visit
3) Always/first/Ravi/ranks/his/class/in
4) In/stock/are/the/frequently/holders/groups
5) a/stock/list/of/make/things/in
6) Peacocks/seen/rarely/we/have
7) Noticed/come/she/most of/that/students/the/school/to/time/on
8) Rude/they/some/are/times
9) Will/disturbing/you/always/see/them/class/the
10) Our/will/problems/we/never/with/discuss/them

ADVERB

Adverbs of Place

Here, there, out, up, everywhere, inside, in, down, aside, outside, away, off, somewhere, to and fro, anywhere, on

A. Exercise

Fill in the blanks using place adverb from the list given above.

1) The children are playing _____.
2) The bicycle has been left _____. Anyone can steal it.
3) I have not seen the cattle grazing _____.
4) The victim fell _____ because it was slippery.
5) After playing the game, shoes should be kept _____.
6) If you want, you can sit _____.
7) These days prices are looking _____.
8) Some years ago, bell bottoms were _____ but these days they are _____.
9) Their house is locked _____ as they have gone.
10) The pendulum of the clock swings _____ and _____.
11) The T.V is _____; please put it _____.
12) Will you please keep this bag _____?
13) The group has been left _____.
14) Your dress is too long; it needs letting _____.
15) The child has gone _____; can you call him?
16) Please come _____ and help me with this work.
17) Stay _____. A car is fast approaching.
18) Get ____; or else you'll get drenched in the rain.
19) Dress _____; we're going to visit some friends.
20) Come _____ and see what's happening.

B. Exercise

Rewrite the following sentences changing underlined adverbs into adverbial phrases.

Chose appropriate phrases – during that time, with carelessness, in a weak manner, at this spot, just at this time, at every place, with great speed, in a good manner, to another place, with, in no time, with good manner, at that place, with happiness, in a good manner.

1) Sheela answered rudely.

   Ans) Sheela answered in a rude manner.
2) David runs fast.
3) Rita is coming now.
4) Such diseases were not common then.
5) The arrow fell here.
6) You can buy it anywhere.
7) The pigeon flies swiftly.
8) Did Kamla behave well?
9) Go away!
10) The dying man replied feebly.
11) He does his work carelessly.
12) Mohan and his friends will come soon.
13) He spoke eloquently.
14) We will pitch the tents there.
15) Although the soldiers were hungry, they marched cheerfully.
16) Does she type properly?
17) I saw them. They were running hurriedly.
18) The door was opened suspiciously.

ADVERB

C. Exercise

Replace adverb phrases into one word adverbs.

1) The bodies were lying in a horrid manner
   Ans) the bodies were lying horridly.
2) Let us stop the work this very moment.
3) It was just on this spot that he died.
4) The child replied with perfect honesty.
5) The guests arrived at that moment.
6) I hope he will come on a very early date.
7) He seemed to have acted with cunningness.
8) I accept your statement without reserve.
9) I thank you with all my heart.
10) He succeeded without any doubt.
11) The window blew with noise.
12) He has proved his case to my satisfaction.

Adverb of Degree or Quantity

Very, too, extremely, temporarily, almost, quite, hardly, more, much, almost, dear, enough, more, little, a few, few

A. Exercise

Fill in the blanks with the adverb of degree or quantity. Degree adverbs can take an adjective, an adverb, present participle.

Note the Example: too cold

1) This book is **very** difficult. (**very**, quietly, extreme)
   Note : Adverb 'very' has taken 'adjective' 'difficult'.

2) The patient is _____ weak. (verily, quite, simply)
3) They have _____ shifted. (temper, temporarily, extremely)
4) There is an _____ river. (extremely, extreme, extremely broad)
5) The beggar has _____ clothes. (few, very few)
6) Students have _____ (quite enough, enough) food.
7) Gold is _____ for me to buy it. (dear, always dear)
8) Sugar is _____ finished. (now, almost)
9) The problem has become _____ difficult. (much more, extreme, quietly)
10) This is a _____ difficult sum. (extremely, very)
11) The crowd is _____ than before. (more, more annoying, much annoying)
12) The manager is _____ disgusted with your work. (enough, extremely, very more)
13) Rahel has _____ completed her project. (now, soon, hardly)
14) The telephone bell rang _____ loudly. (very, quite, too, all)
15) The student needs _____ time. (little more, some more, all, just little more)

Complete the table according to exercise A.

Adverb	Adjective	Present participle-ing Past participle	adverb	verb	Pronoun noun
Very+	Difficult	_____	_____	_____	_____
Quite+	Weak	_____	_____	_____	_____

ADVERB

Temporarily+	___	___	___	Shifted	___	___
Extremely	broad	___	___	___	___	___
___	few	___	___	___	___	clothes
___	___	___	___	___	___	___
Almost, now	___	___	___	finished	___	___
Much, more	Difficult	___	___	___	___	___
___	___	___	___	___	___	sum
more	___	Annoying	___	___	___	___
Extremely	___	Disgusted	___	___	___	Your work
___	___	completed	___	___	___	___
___	___	___	___	___	___	___

Interrogative Adverbs

> What, where, when, why, how whom, which

Note- Use verb+ adverb

Where did you go?

(Ans) I went + to school

1) What did the children want? (to play)
2) Why did he cry? (for food)
3) Where did Simar want to meet you? (at)
4) Where does she keep my clothes? (in)
5) How do you go to office? (by)
6) When does your father comes from office? (at)
7) Which is your complaint? (to)
8) How did the prisoner come out of jail? (by breaking)
9) Where do these poor people live? (near)
10) Why will you not continue to work? (to)

Edit the following sentences. One word is missing. Write the word before and after the missing word. Write the correct word

The dog was playing the children.	a)	_____ _____
When they started throwing stones him,	b)	_____ _____
he started bark. The children got frightened.	c)	_____ _____
and ran fast. The dog	d)	_____ _____
ran them. The children ran as	e)	_____ _____
fast they could but the dog	f)	_____ _____
was faster them.	g)	_____ _____

This blind man walks	a)	_____ _____
but sometimes falls.	b)	_____ _____
Some kind help	c)	_____ _____
him to get, but some do not bother	d)	_____ _____
even turn towards him.	e)	_____ _____
It's pity that some people	f)	_____ _____
not have feelings such helpless people.	g)	_____ _____

Prepositions

Prepositions are placed before nouns, pronouns or noun phrases.

Over, on, in, into, at, off, of by, for, from, through, with, without, among, between, beyond, beside, outside, around etc

---

The word preposition has prefix 'pre' is placed before the word 'preposition'. Preposition is placed before a noun or pronoun.

Example :

Renu put the book on the shelf.

'on' is a preposition, 'the shelf' is a noun.

PREPOSITIONS

A. Exercise

Circle the prepositions and underline the nouns.

1) The plane is flying above the clouds.
2) A taxi passed before a bus.
3) There's a cow in the field.
4) He is fond of tea.
5) The cat jumped off the chair and climbed up the ladder.
6) My purse is in my bag.
7) I know he left before me.
8) Malini lives in London.
9) Ragini is not at home; she has gone to office.
10) Throw it into the garbage bin.
11) The insect is moving on my leg. It is on my bag now?
12) In his fury he fell upon his rival.
13) The old man fell to the ground.
14) Though he deals in branded clothes, he doesn't earn enough.
15) Renu lives with her family.
16) Mr. Raj lives in a small cottage. Even though his cottage is small, his large family enjoys living in it.
17) Dases lived in our neighbourhood, but they left in march this year.
18) When we went to Agra, we met many relatives.
19) I wonder why she doesn't have a taste for music.
20) This group is angry with him for his misbehaviour.
21) Ramola neither agrees with you nor with your proposal.
22) My sister applied to the principal for two days leave.
23) Rohan has competed with his friend for a prize.

Complete the table from the given sentences. Make another chart to work out rest of the sentences.

Preposition	Nouns	Preposition	Nouns
above	the clouds	to	office
before	a bus	into	the garbage in
in	the field	on	my leg
of	tea	on	my bag
up	the ladder	in	his fury
in	my bag	upto	his rival
before	me	to	the ground
in	london	in	branded clothes
at	home		

Preposition shows relation between two things; mostly with a noun or pronoun.

List of Prepositions

Time Preposition- at, on, in, by, to, till, until, during, for, since, from-to, within, before, after etc.

Place preposition- at, in, on, to, across, under, beside, below, beyond, near, above, down,

Into, upon (things in motion)

Agent- by, with

Others- between, among, besides

B. Exercise

Fill up the blanks using correct clue.

1) The dog ran on the road. (on, in, at)
2) The river flows under the bridge. (over, on, under)
3) The work was done _____ haste. (at, in)

PREPOSITIONS

4) He is afraid _____ dogs. (of, with, by)
5) Sushma is fond _____ music.
6) He goes _____ temple _____ Sundays. (in, to, of, on)
7) The soldiers give their lives fighting _____ their country. (with, to, for, about)
8) Mr, Sinha lives _____ Hyderabad _____ Tilak street. (in, on, at)
9) These labourers leave their homes _____ six _____ the morning. (early in, at, during, in)
10) Director, Nek Chand is well known _____ his rock garden. (about, for, upon)
11) That portrait was painted _____ a famous artist (at, by) who achieved fame __ the sixteenth century. (on, in)
12) I must start now _____ reach the station _____ time. (for, to, upon, on)
13) The child has been missing _____ yesterday. (for since, till)
14) The caravan must reach the destination _____ sunset. (within, before, in)
15) Get ready! The train is _____ reach the platform. (up to, about for, about to)
16) Mr Singh does not leave his house _____ 9 o'clock. (before, in, for)
17) The express train departs _____ 3pm _____ Delhi. (on, at, for)
18) I received his message _____ the night. (during, at)
19) _____ rice he had hot curry. (along, with, together)
20) Come and sit _____ me. (with, together)
21) Ordinary people don't have access _____ higher authority. (to, with, along)

22) The criminal is accused _____ several crimes. (by, with, of)
23) People should abstain _____ drugs. (of, in, from)
24) The student has apologized _____ his misbehaviour. (for, about)

Make a table of preposition and the noun it follows

Preposition	Noun	Preposition	Noun
on	road	_____	_____
under	the bridge	_____	_____
_____	haste	_____	_____
_____	dogs	_____	_____
_____	music	_____	_____
to	_____	_____	_____
_____	their country	_____	_____
in	_____	_____	Tilak street
___ six ___	_____	_____	_____
_____	his rock garden	_____	_____
_____	a famous artist	_____	_____
_____	_____	_____	_____

Identify adverbs and prepositions:
C. Exercise
put them in the given table and write whether they are adverbs or preposition. An adverb tells about a verb, an adjective or another adverb. Study the adverb section.

Remember- nouns comes after a verb.

1) Come down.
2) We sailed down the river.

PREPOSITIONS

3) The man walked around the house.
4) The boy sat up.
5) The boy sat on the stool.
6) The carriage moved on.
7) The soldiers passed by.
8) The man turned round.
9) We all went into the room.
10) He hid behind the door.
11) My friends left me behind.
12) The girls sat by the cottage door.
13) The path goes through the woods.
14) I have read the book through.
15) The storm is raging behind.
16) One can't live without water.
17) Go, and run about.
18) My family came the day before yesterday.
19) Is he in this room?
20) The driver jumped off the car.
21) Sit down and relax.
22) Wash your clothes under the tap.
23) The train has slowed down.
24) The pouch slipped off my hand.
25) The child has gone now.
26) The tiger is after its prey.
27) The singer sang at low pitch.
28) The simple couple is cheated by the pick pocket.
29) Have you seen them disappearing in the forest?
30) Kindly take this garbage away.

Write the underlined words under correct headings.

	Preposition	**Adverb**	**Noun**
Down		down	
Down the river	Down		The river
around the house	Around		The house
Up		up	
On the stool			
Moved on			
Passed by			
Turned around			
Into the room			
Behind the door			
Me behind			
By the cottage door			
The book through			
The book through			
Raging behind			
Without water			
Go and run about			
Before yesterday			
In his room			
Off the car			

PREPOSITIONS

D. Exercise

Answer the following questions using appropriate prepositions.

1. Where is the farm?
2. With what do you chop onions?
3. Where do you keep your books?
4. Where do the players play cricket?
5. When will your parents get back?
6. Where is he hiding?
7. What are they watching for into the night?
8. How can I send my letter soon to the manager without any delay?
9. Why couldn't you put up your complaint?
10. Where is the newspaper?
11. Why aren't you accompanied by your companions?
12. Where is the river flowing?
13. Who accompanied you to the air-port?
14. What did your father buy for you?
15. For which exam did your brother sit?

Some prepositions which need to be understood

clearly _____ beside, besides, from- to

beyond, at, on, during, within, between, by

Note:

'Beside' means at the side of.

Example :

The Vase is beside a book.

'Besides' means in addition to.

Example : I have three other hats besides this one.

E. Exercise

1. She has taken a book _____ me.
2. Rahul sits_____ Mohit.
3. The invities will enjoy different activities _____ delicious eatables.
4. _____ Diwali time various unique sweets are available.
5. _____ nine _____ 12 Raju will be giving his exam.
6. _____ Christmas day, Santa Clause distributes gifts.
7. The village is _____ those hills.
8. _____ holidays, people enjoy and relax.
9. Keep yourself _____ limits.
10. Distribute these sweets _____ your two sisters.
11. _____ playing, students should give time to their studies.
12. My elder brother will be in India _____ October _____ March.
13. The grammar book is _____ Geography book.
14. The green grocer's shop is _____ the stationery shop.
15. Good citizens abide _____ law.

Edit the following sentences. There is one mistake in each sentence. Underline the incorrect word and write it correctly in the given space.

1) While a shepherd was going along   a) _____ _____
   his friend, sonu, he told him for   b) _____ _____
   come to his house
   at Monday as his family   c) _____ _____

PREPOSITIONS

would be glad for have   d) _____ _____
him about dinner as   e) _____ _____
they were celebrating his   f) _____ _____
son's sixteenth birthday.   g) _____ _____

2) These students have exam in   a) _____ _____
   Monday. The noise on our   b) _____ _____
   neighbourhood
   Is loud. It is difficult to them   c) _____ _____
   For concentrate in their studies   d) _____ _____
   I am sorry to their problem   e) _____ _____
   Their house is nearer. the noisy   f) _____ _____
   Place. Can somebody tell   g) _____ _____
   them for
   Stop this noise?   h) _____ _____

Prepositions used after different parts of speech like – 'ing' form of the verb, noun, pronoun, possessive adjective, possessive pronoun, etc.

Fill in the blanks using the following expressions or other.

Blame for, accessible to, alliance with, cessation or others from, deliverance from, addicted to, well versed in, contented with, contempt of, accused of, designed for, capacity for, craving for, cautious of, acceptable to, attachment to, descent from, escaped from, adjacent to, of, for, determined to, assured of, etc.

1. The criminal is _____ murdering a man.
2. The designer has designed a beautiful dress _____ you.
3. Just because that man is _____ alcohol, he is unable to take care of his family.
4. This bucket has the _____ holding ten litre of water.

5. Raj said, "My parents are not _____ my result.
6. Mrs. Sunita keeps on munching as she has _____ pan masala.
7. I am _____ his success.
8. My aunt's house is _____ ours.
9. The police are keeping a close watch as a prisoner has _____ the prison.
10. That building beyond those mountains is hardly _____ people.
11. People say, He is well _____ English.
12. I am _____ getting success.
13. These people want _____ their bad habits.
14. Some parties have _____ opposition.
15. These customers are in need _____ some medicines.
16. These boys are _____ misbehaving with their teacher.
17. She is sorry _____ coming late.
18. Your result _____ your hard work.
19. The orders are to escape _____ shooting.
20. One should be well _____ in English to get higher position.
21. That young man is _____ his services
22. Rao is _____ his success.
23. Be _____ this snake.
24. I don't understand why you have _____ this person.
25. This kind of rude behaviour is _____ me.
26. Mothers have great _____ their kids.
27. They are _____ this destruction.
28. The _____ the peak is extremely difficulty

29. _____ drugs is harmful.
30. His _____ school for so many days has put him into trouble.

Answer the following questions using the clues.

Underline the preposition and circle the next word, notice what part of speech it is.

1. When did the meeting begin? (afternoon, at afternoon, in the afternoon)
2. What blew off the roof? (the storm, storm)
3. For whom did they bring the furniture. (us)
4. For whom did the father buy such interesting puzzles? (Children)
5. What did he have to do? (The dates for exam)
6. What did he give up? (smoke)
7. Whom did she call for help? (sister)
8. What did you get back? (our money)
9. Where did the police break into? (the hiding place)
10. What has she broken up? (engagement)
11. What was he made to do? (pay his debts)
12. What does he want you to do? (stop chatting)
13. Which book has the child thrown away? (maths book)
14. Why does the child hide behind the curtain. (because he is timed)
15. For whom is he cooking such delicacies? (especial guests)
16. When will they come out of their office? (at 6 p.m.)
17. Are you interested in reading novels? (yes)
18. Where did this accident take place? (in the road, on the road)
19. With whom do you enjoy parties? (friends)

Join the following sentences using a suitable preposition + -ing form of the verb.

Example :

The thief entered the house. He broke the window.

Ans. The thief entered the house **by breaking** the window.

1. The teacher congratulated the team. It won the match. (on)
2. I will not excuse you. You should take the exam. (from)
3. There is no air. We can't breathe. (without)
4. They secured the house. They locked it. (after)
5. The police fined the cyclist. He cycled at night. The cycle didn't have a map. (without)
6. She reads poetry. She finds great pleasure. (in)
7. Ali wants to catch fish. But he doesn't want to wet his hands. (without)
8. Rajan sleeps in the open. He is used to it (in)
9. Stephan wants to pass the exam. He has set his mind on it. (on)
10. The boys expected to win the match. They pinned their hope on it. (in)
11. The visiting guest was eating fish. He was fed up. (of)
12. They spent hours. They were writing the reports. (in)
13. The volcano erupted. It made an exploding sound (with)
14. The farmers rejoiced. They got good a price for their harvest. (on)
15. I am relieved. I have completed my project. (after)

ARTICLES

Articles 'a', 'an', 'the' are Determiners. They are placed before a noun.

Types of Determiners-

1. Indefinite Articles – a, an
2. Definite Articles – the

Use 'a' when the noun after it begins with a consonant sound. Letters which give vowel sound are a, e, i, o u. All the other letters are consonants. Sometimes some consonants lose their sound. The vowel next to it gives its sound so article 'an' is used. Example An hour. The noun next to it should be singular. Nouns which begin with vowels but don't give vowel sound take 'a' as : a European.

Exercise :

Fill in the blanks using 'a' or 'an'

Note :

Sometimes a noun is preceded by an adjective or an adverb. If the adjective begins with a vowel, use an'

Example :

An intelligent boy

It is a very sweet orange.

Use 'a' or 'an'

_____ book, _____ chair, _____ house, _____ university, _____ European, _____ girl, _____ boy, _____ umbrella,

_____ hour, _____ Indian, _____ engineer, _____ old watch, _____ red tomato, _____ tedious exercise, _____ air conditioned car, _____ Indian university, _____ university, _____ yellow mango, _____ young girl, _____ one rupee note, _____ honest lady, _____ radio, _____ engine, _____ device.

Use 'a' or 'an' in the following situations.

1. When just one of a class is mentioned.

   Example :

   A cow gives milk

   A hen lays eggs

A doctor treats patients.

A cow, A hen and A doctor belong to their own class.

When the listener is not familiar to the person that is mentioned, use 'a'.

Example :

I met a man in the street.

Exercise :

Supply 'a' or 'an' where needed.

1. There is fly in your tea.
2. Can you buy me kilo of sugar.
3. This child has eaten slice of bread.
4. We have lot of space for all your candidates.
5. He drove his car at ninety kilometers hour.
6. I am happy to tell you that my brother has become doctor.
7. It is European university. If you want you can take admission in it.
8. Ramesh picked up mango and ran away.

ARTICLES

9. I had talk with engineer.
10. She's asking for sack of wheat.
11. That customer has bought packs of chocolates.
12. Apple day keeps the doctor away.
13. I have asked my mother to buy me a notebook, pencil, rubber and geometry box.
14. Shall I prepare cup of tea for you?
15. Ravi wants to buy kilo of sugar.
16. How much is litre of oil?
17. Mr. Sahu is lecturer in Our college.
18. Can you please give me packet of envelopes?
19. There is important piece of news.
20. I have bought expensive pair of shoes.

Definite Article

Definite article indicates the noun which is specially identified.

Note the difference

a) I met a lady on my way to school. She is known to my mother-in-law.

b) The lady whom I met on my way to school is known to my mother-in-law.

Explanation (a) A lady can be any lady.
(c) The lady is a specific lady.

When to use definite article

1. Unique single things take 'the' –

The moon, the sun, the sky, the world, the Earth, the Equator, the North Pole, the South Pole, The Bible, the Granth Saheb, the Quran, the Ramayan, etc.

2. When particular persons are known to the speaker and the listener.

   The President, The Prime Minister

3. When attention is attracted towards particular things

   (a) Please give me the book which is on the table.

   The book is a particular thing

   (b) You should put on the dress which you wore last Friday

4. When superlative degree is used

   She is the best singer in our school

   'Best' is superlative degree.

5. When ordinals are used.

   I went through the second chapter and came across some important points.

   Second is an ordinal.

6. When a noun is mentioned the second time. In stories a non can be repeated frequently.

Example :

We saw **a beautiful painting. The painting** attracted many visitors.

Instructions : Fill up the blanks using 'the' if 'the' is not needed put a cross in it.

A. Exercise

1. The man who climbed up the peak has been awarded. (special).
2. _____ milk is necessary for babies. (in general)
3. _____ milk which Sonal bought has spoiled.
4. _____ coffee grown in this state is popular.

ARTICLES

5. _____ coffee is preferred by many people.
6. _____ coffee used to be very strong.
7. _____ rich should not boast.
8. _____ Guptas are out of station.
9. _____ Netherlands, _____ United States of America are plural names.
10. Voting is done in _____ school behind that building.

B. Exercise

Fill in the blanks using 'a', 'an' or 'the'. Put an X where none is needed.

1. There is _____ man waiting outside for you.
2. What are you talking about? I am talking about _____ tragedy which took place in this area.
3. I am going to ask you _____ important question.
4. My husband is _____ writer; most of the time he is seen with his pen and diary.
5. _____ chair in that corner has _____ broken leg, please don't use it.
6. My friend gave me _____ yellow flower. I don't know what its name is.
7. Her uncle is _____ M.P. He visits different organizations.
8. My mother is _____ best cook.
9. Suneeta is _____ honest girl.
10. Rani has bought _____ kilo of rice. _____ rice we have in that container isn't as good as this.
11. _____ lady who lives in that white house is my science teacher.
12. _____ horse gallops, _____ dog doesn't.

13. _____ universe is vast; _____ Earth is just _____ small part of it.
14. _____ camera you presented me, gives good results.
15. Father gave me _____ valuable piece of advice.
16. That man is carrying with him _____ umbrella, _____ walking stick _____ cap and _____ hand bag.
17. This is _____ home of the administrator.
18. I am going _____ home.
19. I met Mr. Raj _____ Principal.
20. _____ student who is usually late has been advised.
21. This hospital has been set up for _____ poor.
22. Anup is called _____ Kalidas of our school.
23. We are expecting _____ Kumars.
24. My children have gone to _____ school.
25. _____ Equator has very high temperature.
26. People live on _____ Earth.

C. Exercise

Supply an article wherever it is needed.

Ravi   _____ sky is clear. Shall we go fishing?
Shanu.   You are right but soon _____ Sun will come out.
Ravi   What should we do then? We shouldn't let _____ day go waste.
Shanu   Let us relax at _____ home.
Ravi.   In that case I'll listen to _____ President's speech.
Shanu: Have you read _____ book our President has written?
Ravi :   No, I haven't but would like to
Shanu :   _____ book you lent me is lengthy.

ARTICLES

Ravi : Of course, you may not like _____ first chapter.

Shanu : Look ! _____ sky is covered with black clouds. It may clear up later. We can go out.

D. Exercise

Put in articles where needed.

Once upon _____ time there was _____ doctor. He worked in his clinic day and night. There was healing touch in his hand. _____ poor _____ rich _____ needy brought their patients only to him. One night while _____ doctor was at his desk _____ old man came to him. His legs shook and he looked very weak. _____ Doctor told him to sit down but _____ old man wouldn't _____ doctor asked _____ patient what his problem was. _____ old man replied that he came to him not for himself but for his wife. He wanted _____ doctor to see his wife at home. _____ old man touched _____ doctor's feet and requested him to accompany him _____ doctor didn't want to go. On seeing _____ man desperate, _____ doctor decided to go with him. _____ old man had come to _____ doctor all the way on foot. _____ doctor took the old man in his car towards _____ lonely hut. _____ doctor wasn't surprised to see _____ hut because he did look very poor. When they reached, _____ hut _____ old lady came staggering. She opened _____ door. _____ doctor and _____ old man entered _____ hut. As soon as they stepped in, _____ ground under their feet sank. _____ doctor's eyes were wide open in fear and surprise. They landed in _____ big palace. _____ Old lady looked like _____ queen and _____ old man like a king. _____ doctor couldn't believe his eyes. He was served _____ best food and was given _____ lot of money to set up _____ big hospital.

DETERMINERS

Just like articles (a, an, the), determiners also determine nouns or pronouns.

There are seven pronouns which work as subject in the English language. Each subject pronoun changes into different forms according to its function as given in the table below.

Subject Pronoun	Object Pronoun	Possessive Adjective Pronoun		Possessive Pronoun	Reflexive Pronoun
I	me	My	N	Mine	myself
He	Him	His		His	Himself
She	Her	Her +	O	Hers	Herself
You	You	Your		Yours	Yourself, yourselves
We	Us	Our	U	Ours	Ourselves
It	It	Its		Its	Itself
they	Them	Their	N	Theirs	Themselves

Examples- different forms of 'I'

I have written these books. 'I' subject

These are <u>my books</u>. Determiner 'my' possessive adjective

These books are <u>mine</u>. Determiner 'mine' possessive pronoun

I have written these books <u>myself</u>. 'myself' reflexive pronoun

(A) Exercise

Complete the following sentences according to the examples given above use the clues.

DETERMINERS

1) She has given the book to them.
   - She has given **her** book to him. (use possessive adjective)
   - She **herself** has given the book to him. (reflexive of 'she')
   - She has given the book to him **herself**. (reflexive of she)

2) He has repaired the tap.
   - He has repaired _____ tap. (possessive of 'they')
   - He has repaired their tap _____. (reflexive of 'he')
   - He _____ has repaired the tap. (reflexive of 'he')

3) You have been interrogating people.
   - You have been interrogating _____ people. (possessive of 'you')
   - You have been interrogating your people _____. (reflexive of 'you')
   - You _____ have been interrogating your people. (reflexive of 'you')

4) We have given them an umbrella.
   - We have given them _____ umbrella.
   - We have given _____.
   - We _____ have given them umbrella.
   - We have given them our umbrella _____.

Note- possessive adjectives and possessive pronouns are working as determiners.

This, that, those, these + noun

These determiners specifically point out the nouns which follow them. Use <u>this or that</u> for the singular noun. Use <u>these, those</u> for plural nouns.

(B) Exercise

Fill in the blanks using correct demonstrative determiners.

1) I would like to take _____ flower; they would like to take _____ flowers.
2) _____ trees need to be cut down but _____ needn't.
3) _____ people who are standing near me aren't to be blamed.
4) I have gone through _____ book. It has a very interesting plot.
5) How long have you known _____ people?
6) _____ are the Sharmas who live near the railway station.
7) If _____ is your point, I will agree with you.
8) The mistress gave me _____ message to be passed to you.
9) We can eat _____ mangoes but not _____ which are on _____ far away table.

C. Quantity Adjectives work like Determiners.

Some, any, much, many, little, a little, few, a few, less, the little, the few etc

Much + uncountable noun- water, oil, butter, rice, hair (on head)

Many + countable noun- pens, books, birds, men etc.

Little- quantity not sufficient – little oil, butter, milk, water- can't be counted

A little – just enough

The little – whatever little quantity was left use uncountable nouns.

Few – used for countable things – few students, few notebooks means not enough for the purpose.

DETERMINERS

Example – We have few tomatoes; this dish requires a lot of tomatoes.

A few – for countable nouns. Means just enough not much.

The few – whatever small things are left.

Example – The few tomatoes we had have been eaten by children.

Some and any

Use 'some' with positive.

Use 'any' in negative.

A question takes 'any'

(C) Exercise

Study the explanation for different determiners given above and then fill in the blanks.

Determiners- some, many, much, any, little, a little, few, a few, the little, the few, more, enough, quite.

1) There is _____ water in the jug, it isn't enough even for one person. If you add _____ water in it, it will suffice. (a little, more, little)

2) Because of rain _____ students have turned up. The teacher can't teach what she has planned. (little, few, a little)

3) _____ biscuits we had, have been eaten away by rats. What can we offer the guests now? (few, a little, the few)

4) There is _____ water in the bucket, please close the tap. (more, much, little)

5) _____ students have come to attend the lecture. You had better get into the classroom. (any, some)

6) Are there _____ customers who want to buy these coats? (any, some)

7) Don't demand _____ ration; you've had enough. (more, enough)
8) This hall is big _____ to accommodate all your guests. (enough, quite)
9) The thirsty man wants _____ water to drink. (most, more)
10) The musician knows _____ about music.

(D) Exercise

Other determiners – all, all of, each, every, both, neither, either, other, a lot of, another, most, several, one, two etc

Fill in the blanks using the determiners given above.

1) _____ people come to watch the program. (one, several, each)
2) Out of all the players only _____ player won the award. (one, all, most of)
3) Write _____ incorrect word twice. (another, each, most)
4) This is the _____ time Rajini has ranked first in her class.
5) The demonstrators are making _____ havoc in the town. (lot, a lot of, much of)
6) _____ of the two students has helped the Head Girl in maintaining discipline. (either, either or)
7) _____ Nirmala nor her friend has brought her English text book. (neither, either, both)
8) You have come now; _____ of the work has been completed. (most, more)
9) Rahul can sit on _____ seat; we are already two sharing the same seat. (another, other, one another)
10) _____ the guests have come; we had better start the program. (a lot, lot, all)

DETERMINERS

11) _____ my father and mother have discussed the situation; we need not worry. (both, either, neither)
12) We saw _____ people standing at the door. (much, any, a lot of)
13) You can take _____ mangoes. (any, one, two)
14) This is the _____ point to be understood. (one, most, first)
15) Amit has been given _____ the answers to his questions. (every, each, all)

ADJECTIVES

An adjective modifies a noun

Examples : red rose, many children, beautiful garden, one mistake, this book, which film, little milk, a little sugar, few books, a few books, beautiful, red, ____ quality adjective

quantity – adjective litter, a little, few, a few, the little, the few, this – demonstrative adjective, One – number adjective which – interrogative adjective

So the type s of a adjectives are

1. Quality Adjectives
2. Quantity Adjective
3. Demonstrative Adjectives
4. Number Adjectives
5. Interrogative Adjectives

1. Quality Adjectives

Some of them are – yellow, white, big, tall, thin, beautiful, bitter, loud, rough, hard, smooth, intelligent, brave, round, wide, short, long, bad, high, heavy, happy, flat, wrong, blue, sweet, . Fill in the blanks using quality adjectives given above.

A. Exercise:

Fill in the blanks using quality adjectives given in the list

Adjectives can be placed before a noun or after a noun in the predicate.

ADJECTIVES

Example : 1. The rich man wanted more and more money.
2. The house **is big**.

1. This soup tastes _____.
2. _____ roads are found in big cities.
3. The _____ teacher was awarded.
4. This noise is _____.
5. That bouquet looks _____.
6. This box is _____.
7. The _____ box is difficult to carry.
8. The _____ soldiers are not afraid to be injured.
9. All the balls are _____
10. _____ wood lasts long.
11. The surface of the table is _____
12. There used to be _____ ceilings some years ago.
13. His bed is _____ that is why his legs are out of the bed.
14. The _____ route will be time consuming for us.
15. This is a _____ example.
16. How can you say it is a _____ decision?
17. The _____ curtains look beautiful.
18. Your _____ dress will attract the attention of the guests.
19. In order to make lemon juice _____ add some sugar in it.
20. _____ students understand the subject Quickly.

2. Quantity Adjectives

Quantity adjectives used with countable nouns

Many, a lot of, few, a few, every, 1, 2, 3, 4 numbers, some, several, the few, a kilo of, a packet of, two cans of, set of, etc.

Note : few – means quantity is equal to nothing.

(a) There are few bunches but the chief guests are more.

(b) There are a few chocolates. They are enough for these ten children.

(c) A lot of can be used both for countable and uncountable nouns.

B. Exercise

Fill in the blanks using quantity adjectives given above. The few means whatever was left has been finished.

1. _____ people have crowded that place.
2. In order to get this dance performance _____ girls and boys are needed.
3. _____ citizen has right to vote.
4. The cat has eaten _____ biscuits we had, we have no more in the house.
5. _____ candidates didn't attend the meeting
6. There were _____ books on that shelf, the librarian expects more books.
7. _____ more students can be admitted in class nine.
8. _____ oil we had, has spilled.
9. Please pour _____ more tea into my cup. (uncountable noun)
10. _____ street dogs are running after a small boy.
11. You have wasted _____ time.
12. _____ tomatoes have been spoiled.

ADJECTIVES

13. Rahel has kept _____ chocolates for herself and _____ for her younger sister.
14. _____ of the wedding cards have been taken to distribute.
15. The school has ordered for _____ Biology books.
16. One _____ oil is needed to cook this dish.
17. _____ students have taken admission; it is a matter of concern.
18. We have _____ photographs, quite many relatives can have them.

3. Demonstrative Adjectives

Following are the demonstrative adjectives – this, that, these, those, such

They point out a definite noun.

Fill in the blanks using correct demonstrative adjective.

Example; This fruit is good. (for singular noun)
These clothes should be worn at special occasions. (for plural nouns)

Those monuments are well known.

These names are to be given to the principal.

Such behavior is not approved.

C. Exercise

Fill in the blanks using demonstrative adjective.

1. I saw many dresses in _____ shop but I liked _____ red one.
2. Can you call up _____ performers? I want to give them some gifts.

3. We saw _____ shoes in one of _____ shops.
4. This is _____ blunt knife, onions can't be chopped with it.
5. _____ group of students will go on picnic next month.
6. Is _____ the only candidate who has turned up for _____ interview?
7. Renu came with _____ problem; I have to help her out.
8. The judge has given such a decision that _____ whole world praises it.
9. After watching _____ light movie, I felt relaxed.
10. _____ flowers are good for decorating the hall.
11. _____ are the clothes they have placed aside.
12. No one will accept _____ a decision.

4. Number Adjectives

These adjectives have cardinal and ordinal numbers. 1, 2, 3, 4 …….. are ordinal numbers. Cardinal numbers are first, second, third (most important on which something depends as The first prize goes to Aman.

D. Exercise

Fill in the blanks using numbers.

1. It is very difficult to choose _____ prize among five hundred competitors.
2. The customer needs _____ pens, _____ note books and _____ atlases.
3. If some body walks up the _____ floor, he becomes breathless.
4. At _____ O'clock our classes begin.
5. There must be _____ people in this crowd.

5. Interrogative Adjective

Which, where, when, who, whom, whose, that

The given adjectives take nouns with them. They are also relative pronouns when are used in complex sentences (adjective clauses)

Examples : Which book do you need? Simple sentence
Whose book is this? Simple sentence
This is the boy who lost his book complex sentence

E. Exercise

Fill in the blanks using interrogative adjective or relative pronouns given above

1. He bought the book _____ he wanted.
2. _____ answer is right?
3. This is the boy _____ was crying for his lost shoes.
4. _____ answer did you give?
5. That is the stranger _____ I saw in the market.
6. At _____ time did you come?
7. I showed him the room _____ is next to the living room.
8. He returned the book _____ I gave him.

Degrees of Comparison

Positive Degree. It describes a noun.

Ravi is an intelligent boy. (Only Ravi's intelligence is described)

Comparative Degree : One noun is compared with another noun.

Ravi is more intelligent than Raj

(two people are compared)

Superlative Degree

Ravi is the most intelligent boy.

Ravi's intelligence is compared with many boys' intelligence)

Examples : Look at the sketches.

1. This boy is short. (A)
2. The boy A is shorter than the boy. (B)
   OR
   The boy B is taller than the boy A.
3. 'C' is the tallest boy. (C) (B) (A)

Note :

1. When two nouns are compared, comparative degree and 'than' are used.

2. When superlative degree is used one noun is compared with three or more than three nouns as it is shown in No. 3 figures.

Rules to form comparative and superlative degrees.

1

Add –'r' and 'st' to adjectives ending in 'e'.

Positive	Comparative	Superlative
Rude	Ruder	Rudest
Wise	Wiser	Wisest
Close	Closer	Closest
Sure	Surer	Surest
Fine	Finer	Finest

ADJECTIVES

2

Double the consonant coming at the end, preceded by one syllable

Positive	Comparative	Superlative
Thin	Thinner	Thinnest
Sad	Sadder	saddest
Fat	Fatter	Fattest
Big	bigger	Biggest

3

Add –er and est

Positive	Comparative	Superlative
Bright	brighter	brightest
High	Higher	Highest
Dear	Dearer	Dearest
Quiet	Quieter	Quietest

4

Adjectives ending in –y, having two syllables

Positive	Comparative	Superlative
Happy	happier	happiest
Pretty	prettier	prettiest
Heavy	heavier	heaviest
Noisy	noisier	noisiest

5

Adjectives which have more than two syllables

Positive	Comparative	Superlative
Beautiful	more beautiful	most beautiful
Courageous	more courageous	most courageous

6

Irregular comparatives

Positive	Comparative	superlative
Good	better	best
Bad	worse	worst
Little	less	least
Much/many	more	most
Far	farther/further	farthest/farthest

F. Exercise

The sentences have a degree of adjective, join or rewrite the given sentences into two other degrees.

1. Ram is a brave boy.

    Answer:

    (A) Ram is braver than his friend.

    (B) Ram is the bravest boy in his team.

2. Rita is the tallest girl in her class.
3. This mango is sweeter than that mango
4. We drove along a long route. The other route is short.
5. It is a difficult exercise.
6. This tree is drier than that tree.
7. This is the most difficult sum.
8. The chemist's shop is near.
9. Your dress is the brightest.
10. These logs of wood are wet.
11. This dress is brighter than that one.

ADJECTIVES

12. Anu's voice is loud. Rani's voice is soft.
13. The campus of your college is clean.
14. This food is healthy.
15. This log of wood is tough.

G. Exercise

Underline adjectives and state what type they are.

1. This much flour is enough.
2. Ten students have opted to perform.
3. I know this situation is serious.
4. My friend gave me some sweets.
5. The cat has drunk a little milk.
6. The gardener has cut down my favourite plant.
7. Five computers were distributed.
8. Which book do you want?
9. The student who sits in the first row is my neighbor.
10. I have counted these students; they are fifty one.
11. The mistake which he made was quite evident.
12. In this race several people are participating
13. His friend gave that little child all the help.
14. The old man fell to the ground.
15. All the workers are expected to do their work conscientiously.
16. The sky is blue and the stars are bright.
17. We have enough bread to feed ten people.
18. I don't have any extra pen.

Formation of Adjectives

1. Nouns change into adjectives

Nouns	Adjective
Wisdom	wise
Care	careful
Rudeness	rude
Width	wide
Fatness	fat

2. Adverb change into adjectives

Adverb	Adjective	Adverb	Adjective
Promptly	prompt	quickly	quick
Courageously	courageous	bravely	brave
Proudly	proud	smartly	smart
Extremely	extreme	properly	proper
Independently	independent	immediately	immediate

Note :
   a. I have scarcely seen any lions in this forest. scarcely – adverb
   b. Lions are scarce in this forest. Scarce - adjective
   c. We visit them rarely. Rarely – adverb
   d. Our visits to them are rare. Rare – adjective.

Functional Shift or Nominalisation

Rewrite the following sentences, change the words given in brackets, into a noun, adverb, verb or adjective; keep in mind 'tenses'.

ADJECTIVES

1. One needs patience when one is opposed by others. (verb patient)
2. In order to exist one has to work. (noun-existence)
3. I received this information from a reliable person. (verb – informed).
4. Tom rejected whatever we proposed. (noun – proposal.
5. The shopkeeper made an agreement, to supply us with fire wood. (verb-agree)
6. Raju can't get admission without his testimonials. (verb – admit)
7. Rohit has no intention of getting into engineering. (verb – intend)
8. He got success in all his undertaking. (verb – succeed)
9. These mangoes have sweet smell but taste sour.(verb – smell)
10. It is believed that he was the greatest general of the century. (noun form – belief)
11. Before I pay you what is due, you must sign this receipt. (noun – signature)
12. The officer was dismissed for negligence rather than competence. (verb – neglect)
13. He broke the rules without intention. (adverb – unintentionally)
14. His punishment was wrong. (adverb – wrongly)
15. The doctor's mistake was evident. (adverb- evidently)
16. There are long queues in front of oil shops as there is scarcely any oil. (lengthy, scarce)
17. Rohan was brilliant when he was interviewed. (brilliance)
18. Raghav is known for his boldness. (adjective – bold)

19. Ramu is a brave fighter. (verb – fight)
20. Mr. Das manages his company wisely. (noun-manager)
21. He was rude to the principal so he has been punished (noun – rude)
22. The orator addressed the audience with confidence (adverb-confidently).
23. The workers like to work under him because he is a kind director. (adverb-kindly)
24. I am happy to declare that he is a sincere adviser. (adverb – sincerely)
25. The needy go to him as he is a sincere helper. (noun-sincerity)
26. The director is a diligent care-taker of the institute. (adverb – diligently)
27. Dishonest dealers fail to attract customers. (noun – dishonesty)
28. They never fail to invite Jim to their party as he is a pleasant entertainer. (verb - entertains, adverb - pleasantly)
29. Cheerful doners are requested to com-forwarded to make their contribution for the flood victims.(adverb – cheerfully)
30. Only few people can be honest selectors of the capable candidates. (adverb + honestly)

Transformation of sentences
Simple sentences combined into one simple sentence

Note:
The following verbs change as given below -

<u>Was tired, were tired, is tired, am tired, are tired</u>

ADJECTIVES

1. **Change :** The underlined verbs change into being. The next verb tired doesn't change. Example : **'being tired'**

   Two actions are almost simultaneous.

2. **Change :** Singular verbs like walk, take, stand, raise change into 'ing' form.

   Example : Standing behind a tree, the photographer clicked some photographs.

   Note : Two actions are simultaneous – standing and clicked.

3. **Change :** (A) Verbs like has, have, + ploughed

   The farmer has ploughed the field. He will sow the seed.

   Answer: <u>**Having ploughed**</u> the field, the farmer sowed the seeds.

   The sentence means: after ploughing the field, the farmer sowed the seeds.

   (C) Simple past tense verb also changes into having +past participle

   Example: He did his homework. He went to play.

   Answer : Having done his homework, he went to play.

   Means : After completing his homework, he went to play.

A. Exercise :

Combine these sentences into one simple sentence.

1. The student finished his paper. He gave it to the invigilator.

   Answer : Having finished his paper, the student gave it to the invigilator.

2. I took a bath. I went to school.
3. Amit did his home-task. Amit watched a movie.
4. The hunter raised his gun. The hunter aimed at the lion.
5. I walked around the field. I saw a snake.

6. She was standing in front of her house. She heard a horrible sound.

7. He has been cheated once. He is more careful now.

8. The man was wanted by the police. He lay in hiding.

9. He has been invited to speak on annual function of the college. He is preparing his speech.

10. The king had been betrayed by his ministers. He had to yield to his enemy.

11. The prisoner was charged with murder. He pleaded not guilty.

12. The house was decorated with colourful lights. It looked beautiful.

13. The goods had been damaged. They had to be sold at a cheaper rate.

14. He had been dismissed from his post. He couldn't get another job.

15. The house had been repaired. The owners moved in.

16. My bicycle had been stolen. I had to go to school on foot.

B. Use absolute phrase make one simple sentence.

Note : When subjects of two simple sentences are different mention both the subjects.

Example : The sun rose. We went out for a walk.

Ans : The Sun having risen, we went out for a walk

B. Exercise :

1. It is very hot. We can not continue our journey.

    Answer : It being very hot, we can not continue our journey.

2. His house has fallen down. He lives in the out house.

ADJECTIVES

3. The weather was fine. We went on a picnic.
4. Mother got worried for my younger brother. We went out in his search.
5. The bell rang. The boys ran out.
6. The match was over. The players sat down to rest.
7. The match was over. The winning players were given their awards.
8. The battle started. The soldiers went to the battle field.
9. The dinner was brought. The guests began to serve their food.
10. The ship sank. The crew were drowned.

C. Use infinitive to make simple sentences to make one simple sentence.

Example : I want to go to the city. I have to buy furniture.

Answer : I want to go to the city to buy furniture.

C. Exercise:

1. He has two sons. He must educate them.

   Answer : He has two sons to educate.
2. She is very weak. She can not walk.
3. My father was pleased. He heard of my success.
4. He is too weak. He can't walk. (too – to)
5. The farmer has gone to his field. He should do his of work.
6. It is our duty. We must not throw garbage here and there.
7. The dog has sat at the threshold. He must guard the house.
8. The doctor has advised the patient. He ought not to smoke.

9. The factory workers must work hard. Their income will increase.
10. The tiger ran. He had to catch the prey.

D. Use preposition with a noun or a gerund to make one simple sentence.

Example : Join the following sentences

He heard of his success. He was very happy.

Answer: On hearing of his success, he was very happy.

Prepositions on, by, besides, without, since, in spite of, despite, with.

D. Exercise

1. He sold fruit. In this way he earned his living.
2. He wrote a letter. He wrote it with his favourite pen.
3. Gopal is poor. Gopal is honest.
4. Her mother died. She heard the news. She felt extremely grieved. Begin with 'on hearing'.
5. Renu could not go to school. Renu was ill.
6. I helped my friend. Otherwise, he would have been ruined.
7. They were defeated. They were very much disappointed.
8. Ajay saved the child. Ajay risked his life.
9. He dressed my wounds. He also paid for my medication.
10. Neeraj is lazy. Neeraj completes his work on time. (Two answers)

E. Use a non or a phrase in apposition to make one simple sentence.

Example : Join the following sentences into one simple sentence.

ADJECTIVES

Midas was a foolish King. He loved gold more than anything.

Answer: Midas, the foolish king loved gold more than anything.

E. Exercise

1. Delhi is the capital of India. It holds political meetings.
2. Shakespeare was a great literary figure. He wrote many dramas.
3. Tagore was a great poet. He is popular all over the world.
4. Edison invented gramophone. Edison was an American.
5. Wordsworth was born in 1770. He was a great English poet.

F. Use adverbs or adverbial phrases or adjective to join the following sentences into one simple sentence.

Example : He is **honest**. His honesty is **perfect**.

Answer: 1. He is **perfectly honest**. Phrase
2. He is quite honest. Quite (adverb, honest adjective)

F. Exercise

1. He was wounded. His wound was **fatal**.

   Answer : He was fatally wounded.
2. He failed in the examination. It was **unfortunate**.
3. It is sunset. The trees appear **dim**.
4. He will rank first. This is **certain**.
5. Rohan was absent from school. His absence was **intentional**.
6. Mohan refused to help his friend. Mohan's refusal was **firm**.
7. The team reached the playground. They were **punctual**.

8. The dedicated soldier fought. The soldier was **ferocious**.
9. I met my old friend. It was **incidental**.
10. My grandfather will help me. It is **sure**.
11. This sentence is right. This is **undoubted**.
12. The script will be given to actors. It is **clear**. They know it.
13. The gifts have been bought. The children will be **happy** to receive them.
14. Cats like to eat rats. They have **voracious** appetite for them.

Transformation of different types of sentences
Transform the following types of sentences

1. Conditional Sentences :

Note : When 'if clause' has simple past tense, it can be changed into the following ways:

1. If he advised his son, he would improve.
   a. Were he to advise his son, he would improve.
   b. The father did not advise the son so he did not improve.
2. If they had liked the place. They would have gone there again.
   a. Had they liked the place, they would have gone there again.
   b. They did not go there as they didn't like the place.

Exercise : Group A
Write the meaning of the given sentences

1. If they planted more trees, there would be less erosion.
2. Your friend wouldn't go there if you warned him.

3. They would watch that film if they had time.
4. The house would look attractive if they arranged the furniture in a better way.
5. The child would grow healthy if the parents looked after him properly.
6. The fire wouldn't spread so fast if they did not smoke cigarettes on dry grass.
7. If the student studied well, he would not score such low marks.
8. If he robbed the man, he would get the money.
9. If she cheated in the exam, she would be caught.
10. If he went to the green grocer, he would buy some vegetables.

Group B

When if clause has imaginary meaning, 'be' verb is changed into 'were'.

Example : If I were a bird, I would fly in the sky.

Meaning : (a) Were I a bird, I would fly in the sky.
(b) I was not a bird so I didn't fly in the sky.

Exercise B

Give the meaning of the given imaginary sentences.
1. If he were a doctor, he would heal me.
2. If Raj were a robot, he would not depend upon people.
3. Were the magician truthful that he could make the dead alive, he would give life to dead people.
4. Thomas said, "If I were the king I would lead my kingdom peacefully."
5. If I were a mango tree, I would yield the best quality of mangoes.

6. If he were blind, he would experience many difficult situations.
7. If the hare were a tortoise, it wouldn't run fast.
8. If he were a crocodile, he would be extremely dangerous.

Group C

Note : Try to understand the meaning of the given sentence.

a. If he had right understanding, he wouldn't be trapped.
b. Had he right understanding, he wouldn't be trapped.
   Meaning : Both the sentence mean
c. He didn't have right understanding so he was trapped.

Exercise C

Write the meaning of the given sentences as given above in group 'C'.

1. If they had imported more items like these, they would have made more profit.
2. The doctor would have diagnosed the disease if the patient had submitted his different reports of blood, urine and X-ray.
3. The crops would have been harvested if they had bright Sun-shine.
4. I would change many things if I had a magic wand.
5. If I had wings like a butterfly, I would suck nectar from flower to flower.
6. The architect would design magnificent villas if he had a lot of money.
7. If he had interest in reading newspaper daily, he would know what is happening in the world.
8. If he had a spare pen, he would definitely lend me one.

ADJECTIVES

9. He would not beg if he had money for his livelihood.
10. If he had confidence, he would pass in the interview.

Turning 'If not' clauses into 'unless clauses'

Explanation : If not means 'unless'

Example

(a) If he does not pay attention to his studies, he may lose his rank.

Unless

(b) unless he pays attention to his studies, he may lose his rank.

Exercise A

Rewrite the following sentences using 'unless'.

1. If you don't take this route, you will reach there late.
2. If you didn't break the window, your father wouldn't punish you.
3. If this group hadn't taken the taxi, they wouldn't have had the opportunity to see the President and listen to his speech.
4. If the child he doesn't have acute pain in his stomach, he will not cry continuously for so long.
5. If the people don't take proper exercise, breathe in clean air and don't eat balanced diet, they can't be healthy.
6. The shopkeeper will lose his customers, if he isn't well behaved.
7. The farmer wouldn't have had a good crop, if he had not worked hard.
8. The tailor would not give the stitched clothes to his customers on time if he did not work with dedication.

Exercise B

Rewrite the following sentences using 'if not'

1. Unless every student submits his note book the teacher will not know whether the students are doing each day's work.
2. Unless you had created the problem, you wouldn't have been in such a serious trouble.
3. Unless the captain instructs you not to do so, don't follow these changes.
4. We won't need to leave early unless there is shortage of transport.
5. Unless there was interesting programme, the guests would not enjoy it.
6. Unless Rahul tasted this fruit, he wouldn't know how tasty it is.
7. You can't take these things unless you make the payment.
8. These people will not have joy ride on the back of this elephant unless he is fed well.
9. These fruits don't ripe unless there is appropriate weather conditions.

Note : Follow the given structure to keep track of tenses in each clause.

<u>Subordinate Clause</u>	<u>main clause</u>
1. **If clause verb**	**V**
Simple Present Tense	<u>Can</u>, will

Example
(If he **studies** seriously, he **can pass**).

| Present continuous tense | May, shall / + simple present |
| Present perfect tense | Ought to |

ADJECTIVES

    Present perfect   Simple present
    continuous tense

2. **If clause Verb**   <u>**Verb**</u>

   Simple past tense   <u>**could**</u>

   Example :
   If he <u>**worked**</u> hard, he <u>**could pass**</u>.
                         Would
                         Might
                         Should
                         Simple past

3. **If clause verb**   **Verb**

   Past Perfect tense   could have +

   Example
   If he <u>**had worked**</u> hard, he <u>**would have**</u> passed
                         Would have +
                         Might have +   Past participle
                         Should have +
                         Past perfect +

Examples :

1. If father is free, we will visit our aunt.
2. If father was free, we would visit our aunt.
3. If father had been free, we would have visited our aunt.

AS LONG AS

Join the following sentences using 'as long as'.

Example :

I will lend you any amount of money.

Only return it on time.

Answer :

I will lend you any amount of money as long as you return it on time.

1. The doctor says, "I can eat anything. Only I should not eat too much."
2. A thief stole a simple old man's money box. The old man said, "Let him have the box, after all, I have the key."
3. Have no fear; always do the right.
4. You can do skating. Use protective measures.
5. The captain told the players they could go to play. Only follow the rules and keep alert.
6. You can take my book. Only return it after two days promptly.

SO AND ALSO

Join the following sentences using 'so' and 'also'.

Example :

They went to Agra. We went to Agra.

Ans. : (a) They went to Agra and we did also.
 (b) They went to Agra and so did we.

1. She is taking part in the drama. I am taking part in the drama.
2. Rita understands the lesson. Mary understands the lesson.
3. Anil used to teach this class. Suneeta used to teach this class.
4. They reached the airport on time. We reached the airport on time.
5. We are invited to Aman's birthday party.

    They are invited to Aman's birthday party.
6. I have done my homework. Mini has done her homework.
7. I can play football. My brother can play football.
8. He is reading a novel. His sister is reading a novel.
9. Jane gave the correct answer. Renuka gave the correct answer.
10. We played indoor games. They played indoor games.

EITHER AND NEITHER

Rewrite the given sentences using 'either' and 'neither'

Example :
She didn't do the homework and I didn't do the homework.

Ans.: (a) She didn't do the homework and I didn't either.
(b) She didn't do the homework and neither did I.

1. We won't be absent and my friends won't be absent.
2. He doesn't care much and she doesn't care much.
3. Amita is not going out and his sister is not going out.
4. We don't watch many films and they don't watch many films.
5. You won't enjoy this book and she won't enjoy this film.

INVERSION OF SENTENCES

These sentences indicate emphasis.

Example :
We rarely go to watch movies.

Inversion:
<u>Rarely do we go</u> to watch movies.

Note :
Notice the structure 'rarely' is placed first and the given verb is changed into question form.

Exercise :
Give inversion form of the following sentences. Use the underlined words in the beginning of the sentences.

1. They came out **only when** you gave the signal.
2. They had **no sooner** knocked on the door than they ran away.
3. They were ready to listen to us **on no account**.
4. The soldiers marched **forward**.
5. The team is going **there**.
6. The champion is coming **here**.
7. **Only in this way** the police arrested the criminal.
8. The test is **so difficult** that I can't score high marks.

9. The puppets went **up and down**.
10. These days we **seldom** see them.
11. The patient has **hardly** eaten anything.
12. They have **scarcely** seen this animal.

Use of auxiliary verbs for certain expression.
Note :
Auxiliary notes give tense to the verb and make it negative.

If the given verb is affirmative, use negative verb form in contracted structure for the blank space.

Example :
I **won't** be able to come but she **will**.

They **will** be able to come but she **won't**.

Exercice :

1. He will arrive but I _____.
2. He liked the movie but my friends _____.
3. She knows him well but you _____.
4. Anupam didn't pass the test but his sister _____.
5. Neha prepared delicious dishes but Shirin _____.
6. Sunidhi wouldn't accompany you but I _____.
7. Rahul should take up the issue but she _____.
8. The head girl is going to lead but the head boy _____.
9. The captain was not there but his assistant _____.
10. She may be exempted but he _____.
11. This dog will eat that food but that _____.

INVERSION OF SENTENCES

12. Team 'A' might be awarded but team 'B' _____.
13. The chief succeeded in accomplishing his aim but his assistant _____.
14. Raj has swum across the English channel but Robert _____.
15. You have received the invitation cards but we _____.

QUESTION TAG

Give question tags for the following sentences.

Note : The negative verb changes into positive (affirmative verb) and affirmative verb changes into negative verb.

Examples :
Tarika **left** for America two weeks ago, **didn't** she?
Tarika **didn't** leave for America two weeks ago, **did** she?

1. She is a very reserved girl, _____?
2. Many students are absent today, _____?
3. You wrote those letters, _____?
4. There won't be traffic jams, _____?
5. Helen brought the message, _____?
6. These people will help you, _____?
7. The performers sit there, _____?
8. It was a good movie, _____?
9. Mr. Jacob has been your teacher for many years, _____?
10. The plane took off on time, _____?
11. Sudershan left a message for you, _____?
12. You have had your lunch, _____?
13. He is not a dependable person, _____?
14. A bicycle fell on Neeraj, _____?

QUESTION TAG

15. A snake lays eggs as a tortoise does, _____?
16. The Earth goes round the Sun, _____?
17. Plants need food, water and air, _____?
18. Students leave school at 2 p.m., _____?
19. She says so, _____?
20. Those days my friends studied for many hours, _____?
21. I am hare, _____?
22. She put the books on shelves _____?
23. During marriages the relatives of the bride keep very busy, _____?
24. When I got off the bus, I met a stranger, _____?
25. The naughty boy broke the frame of a picture, _____?
26. They bathed in the river, _____?
27. She saw those photographs, _____?
28. Father had a lot of work to complete, _____?
29. Because it is late, we can't play more, _____?
30. Students should come to school in uniform, _____?
31. Some people are used to eating only rice, _____?
32. Even if I insisted, he wouldn't listen to me, _____?
33. When he is angry, he behaves in a funny way, _____?
34. These parents discipline their children, _____?
35. The injured man cried a lot, _____?
36. The kite flew high up, _____?
37. The cricketer struck the ball too high, _____?
38. He plucks fruit without permission, _____?
39. Every body congratulated the player, _____?
40. The painter has painted the scenery beautifully, _____?

ADJECTIVES AS PLURAL NOUNS

Adjectives used as plural nouns

Note : The differences among the following sentences.

(a) The blind **man needs** somebody to guide him.

(b) The blind **men need** some people to help them.

Difference : When the word 'blind' is used to show blind community, it takes a plural verb. The article 'the' is always used with it.

Example :

The **blind need** to be guided. ✓

The blind needs to be guided. ✗

If 'blind' has a noun singular or plural, the verb has to be according to it.

Example :

The blind man needs help.

The blind men need help.

ADJECTIVES AS PLURAL NOUNS

Fill in the blank using the given verbs in simple present tense correctly. Use 'be' verb.

1. The cautious men **aren't** always trapped. (be verb is, aren't, am, are)
2. The cautious man **is** trapped sometimes.
3. The cautious **are** ('be' verb) sometimes trapped.

Rewrite the following sentences in three forms as given above.

4. The rich man _____ (not know) how the poor people _____ (live, lives)
5. The rich boys _____ (not know) how the poor boys _____ (live, lives)
6. The rich merchant _____ (not know) how the poor shopkeepers _____ (live, lives)
7. The meek people _____ (be) always blessed.
8. The meek _____ always blessed.
9. This mean man _____ 'be' is always cheerful.
10. The wicked _____ (flee, flees) when no man pursueth but the righteous people _____ (be) bold.
11. The wicked people _____ (flee, flees) when no man pursueth but the righteous _____ (be) bold.
12. The lame I _____ (have, has) difficulty in going from place to place.
13. This lame man _____ (have, has) difficulty in moving from place to place.

ADJECTIVES AS NOUNS

The following sentences are right or wrong. Put the mark ✓ or ✗. Write the wrong sentences correctly.

1. The poor man looks for help.
2. I have seen the rich <u>boast</u> over <u>their</u> riches. wrong
3. You can send him to a school for blind; the blinds learns everything as a normal person learns.
4. The rich likes to have luxury.
5. A rich man pass by our house quite often.
6. Needy needs not beg; they should earn their living.
7. The wicked witch destroy good things.
8. We must keep away from the wicked as he likes to harm others.
9. The brave men has courage.
10. The brave has courage.
11. A brave man have courage.
12. The blind is quite educated.
13. The blind men are quite educated due to modern technology.
14. The poor is lagging behind.
15. The poor people is lagging behind.
16. The poor man is lagging behind.

ADJECTIVES AS NOUNS

Note : Most of the sentences are wrong with two three mistakes.

Prefixes

When the root word takes some letters before it, those letters are called prefix and the meaning of the root word changes.

Exercise : Add prefix to the given words., literate, legitimate, spell, move, logical satisfy, moral, necessary, natural, mature, regular, legal, pure, advantage, flexible, secure, important, handle, balance.

Use appropriate prefix for the given words.

il, im, un, ir, dis, un, in, mis

Fill in the blanks using the given root words and with their prefixes.

1. We should drink _____ water, _____ water makes us sick.
2. The _____ of depositing our money in bank account is that we get interest on it. The _____ of not depositing our money in our bank account is the amount remains the same.
3. I have kept the _____ papers carefully but the _____ papers are dumped into the waste paper basket.
4. Rubber bands are _____ but hard plastic is _____.
5. People feel _____ in their houses but when there are quarrelsome people on the road, they feel _____.
6. Sometimes adults look _____ as their talks are sensible but sometime _____.

7. They property of a father goes to his _____ son, not to an _____ son.

8. If you _____ your computer carefully, it will work for you perfectly if you _____ it, you will be in problem.

9. _____ workers attend to their duties daily but _____ workers absent themselves quite often.

10. Their reasoning is _____. Since it isn't _____ we can resolve this problem.

11. Our _____ duty is to respect our elders, if we don't and use abusive language, we become _____.

12. Mostly you _____ your words correctly, but this time there are a few words which are _____

13. My mother is always _____ with my result but this time she is _____ as my rank has gone down.

14. Why are you wasting your time on this _____ work? You had better do some _____ work.

Suffix

When letters are added to the root word, they are called suffix. They are added at the end of the word.

Exercise : Add suffix to the given words.

Important, immense, achieve, beauty, impress, remove, please, mischief, confuse, decorate, require, liquidate, promote, cloud, imagine, explain, rain, declare, celebrate, anticipate, ignore, speak, congratulate, construct, humiliate, confront, award, encourage, satisfy

Add correct suffix to the words given above.

ADJECTIVES AS NOUNS

Suffix : tion, -ed, - ation, -y, -al, -ant, -ous, -sion, -ance, -ly, -ment, -ive, -ful, -ary

Fill in the blanks using root words and those words with their suffix.

1. The builders _____ half the building; I don't understand why they don't complete the _____ part.
2. These young boys always _____ their victory. Their _____ are with great enthusiasm.
3. It is sad when a company _____. Because of _____ they have become bankrupt.
4. Please _____ these dirty sports. After their _____ the car will have its shine.
5. Come with us, the weather is _____.
6. The management is going to _____ him. It is worth _____ him.
7. Our teacher always _____ us after our successful performance. Don't you think _____ boosts up one's confidence?
8. This charity organization _____ five hundred blankets; some more can be the _____.
9. When _____ harms somebody, we should get rid of it, but there are some _____ people who keep on hurting people.
10. _____ yourself to be an _____ robot, what all would you wish to do?
11. There is _____ work to be completed. After they have completed their task _____, they will be happy.
12. There is a lot of _____ in this room; please don't _____ me.

13. We _____ good results but your performance is negative.
14. Constant _____ affects one's personality. Please learn not to _____ people.
15. Please don't _____ me when you are with your friend _____ in such situations humiliates a person.

Prefixes and Suffixes

Fill in the blanks using the given words with prefixes or suffixes.

1. The _____ (depart) time of the flight is 10:00 a.m. and the _____ (arrive) time of the other flight is from 11:00 a.m.
2. Those roads were _____ (broad) than these.
3. There are _____ (cheap) items in this shop. In other shops all the items are _____ (cost)
4. Walk _____ (slow) as the path is _____ (mud)
5. The moon looks _____ (dim) these nights but on full moon night it is _____ (bright)
6. The _____ (wrestle) confronted his opponent _____ (sharp)
7. Iron is _____ (heavy) but tin is _____ (light).
8. The _____ (fast) you walk; the _____ (soon) you reach your destination.
9. Because of _____ (agree), they are not able to come to any _____ (agree).
10. Because Rahul _____ (obey) his parents, he was not given the birthday gift.
11. This tree is _____ (short) than that tree.
12. I will call him _____ (immediate) if there is an _____ (urgent).

ADJECTIVES AS NOUNS

Mixture of sentences with certain meanings

Exercise : Give the meaning of the given sentences.

Example; Thieves broke into the house. (force)
Thieves got into the house forcefully.

1. They did honest work. (not honest)
2. My friends have interesting books. (not boring)
3. Anita comes to school regularly (not absent)
4. These children like to play in door games. They ____. (outdoor games)
5. The monitor was too kind to report to the teacher. (so – that)
6. She is too shy to ask a question. (so – that)
7. This news is too good to be true. (so --- that)
8. I was too ill to go to school yesterday.
9. The work is so much that it can't be finished in a single day.
10. He is greater than I am.
11. I am taller than he.
12. I am not less intelligent than my brother.
13. This is the biggest aeroplane I have ever seen. (such)
14. There is little hope of his survival..

Exercise :

Change the negative sentences into positive form.

1. He did not live many years in Europe. (few)
2. There is nobody who believes in his honesty.
3. <u>No one</u> can <u>deny</u> that she is a pretty girl.
   (Change the underline words)

4. God will not forget the cry of the humble.
5. There was no one present who did not cheer.
6. Those students didn't do their work.
7. We are not happy.
8. This work is so difficult that I can not do it.

Give positive assurance to the given sentences.

Virtue is its own reward.
Ans : Isn't virtue its own reward?

1. It does not matter if he fails to come.
2. We were not sent into the world simply to make money.
3. Their glory can never fade (question form, change never)
4. He is unfit for this job.
5. He was a villain to do such a deed. (only)
6. No one can be expected to submit for ever to injustice.
7. There is nothing better than busy life.
8. No where in the world will you find such a noble man.
9. It is useless to offer bread to a man who is dying of thirst.
10. We could have done nothing without your help.

Note : Most of the sentences will change into question and negative words into positive form.

Exclamatory sentences changed into statements

Change the following exclamatory sentences into assertive statement.

Example : What an interesting book !
Answer. It is an interesting book.

ADJECTIVES AS NOUNS

Exercise :

1. O for a cup of water ! (wish)
2. If only I could gain the first prize ! (earnest desire)
3. Alas that he died so young !
4. How incredulous ! you are afraid of climbing up the hill. (surprising)
5. How well she sings !
6. What an intelligent student he is !
7. What a lovely scene !
8. What a mean fellow !
9. Alas ! How extravagant I have been.
10. May you live long !

Exercise:

Change the given assertive sentence into exclamatory sentences.

Question: The night is very cold.
Answer: How cold the night is !

1. He has done his job well.
2. I was grieved to hear the sad news.
3. I was very excited to hear the good news.
4. It was extremely a nasty fall.
5. It is a very pleasant morning.
6. The bird is very pretty.
7. She sings so well.
8. This mountain is very high.
9. The moonlight sleeps so sweetly on this bank.
10. I am ruined. (alas)

11. We have won the match. (Hurrah!)
12. I wish the king lived long.
13. I wish god poured on you his choicest blessings.
14. I wish my friend were here.
15. I wish I were a freeman.
16. I wish God pardoned this sinner.

CLIMATE CHANGE – A MYTH OR A REALITY?

Just today while browsing through some tweets, an Article appearing in Huffington Post Green, dated July 31st caught my attention. The article titled, "Kivalina's Climate Change problem – Why The Small Alaskan Village is Disappearing", described how climate change and rising sea levels are threatening the very existence of the village ! The opening lines read, " It is already difficult to find Kivalina on a map, but soon it may be impossible. Not only does the Alaskan village only cover 1.9 square miles of land (while being) home to less than 400 residents, but it is disappearing. Fast. As one of the most apparent and shocking examples of coastal erosion, Kivalina could be uninhabitable by 2025 – all thanks to climate change." A summary of a five minutes video clip in the Huffington post reads, "Narrated in the Inuits' native tongue, the 5-minute clip shows a quick, tragic peek into the residents' plight. "It's just global warming, " one villager says in the video. "I mean, it's a lot warmer today than it used to be before."

How then could the fate of Kivalina affect those of us who live many thousands of miles away in India? Well I guess whatever is happening in a distant land is a warning of what everyone in the world can expect in times to come. Nations and people closest to the polar ice packs are affected sooner than those that are more removed from them in terms of distance. But then, can we afford to be complacent in the knowledge that we still have borrowed time?

Another story about Global warming revolves around the island nation of Kiribati. This is a low-lying Island Nation located in the central tropical Pacific Ocean. With a population of over 100, 000, its very existence is threatened by rising ocean levels caused by a meltdown of polar ice. The whole populace of Kiribati is looking for an alternate settlement in Australia, the nearest landmass. The Government of Kiribati would have to purchase land in Australia, which I believe is under way !

Popular tourist destinations like the Maldives, Mauritius and Seychelles located in the Indian Ocean, are also threatened by rising ocean levels. It would however, be wrong to conclude that it is only island nations that are affected by rising ocean levels, in fact countries with coastlines too are vulnerable to rising sea-levels!

Countries that have an extensive coastline will be most affected by rising ocean levels – imagine the strain of resettling the entire population of people living in coastal areas. India's coastline stretches over 5700 kilometers on the mainland and about 7500 km including the two island territories. The impact of global warming-induced sea level rise due to thermal expansion of near surface ocean water has great significance for India due to its extensive low-lying densely populated coastal zone. "Sea level rise is likely to result in loss of land due to submergence of coastal areas, inland extension of saline intrusion and ground water contamination which may in turn have wide economic, cultural and ecological repercussions. Observations suggest that the sea level has risen at a rate of 2.5 mm a year along the Indian coastline since 1950s. A mean sea level rise of between 15 and 38 cm is projected by the mid – 21st century along India's coast. Added to this, a 15% projected increase in intensity of tropical cyclones would significantly enhance the vulnerability of populations living in cyclone prone coastal regions of India. Other sectors vulnerable to the climate change include freshwater resources, industry, agriculture, fisheries, tourism and human settlements. Given that many climate change impacts on India's coastal zone feature irreversible effects, the appropriate national policy response should enhance the resilience and adaptation potential of these areas. India has been identified as one amongst 27 countries which are most vulnerable to the impacts of global warming related accelerated sea level rise (UNEP, 1989). The high degree of vulnerability of Indian coasts can be mainly attributed to extensive low-lying coastal area, high population density, frequent occurrence of cyclones and storms, high rate of coastal environmental degradation on account of pollution and non-sustainable development. Most of the people residing in coastal zones are directly on natural resource bases of coastal ecosystems. (**Any global warming-induced climatic change"** *http://in.answers.yahoo.com/question/index?quid=20070326134710AAFPXMQ*.) Can we then sit complacently in our living rooms, secure in the knowledge of the fact that we are far away from the coastline and perhaps less likely to be affected by a deluge of ocean water? The answer is perhaps a strong no! The pressure caused by shifting a large population living in coastal areas both in monetary terms and the physical impact can only be guessed ! The cost of moving the 400 residents of Kivalini is about $400 million, an amount the government has yet to offer! How much more would it cost the Indian Government to shift millions of residents from coastal areas to higher ground? The figures would surely be staggeringly prohibitive !

The global impact of rehabilitating populations of people affected by rising ocean levels would lead to a global economic meltdown! In an age where the ecosystem is already challenged by an increasing population, increased population density caused by the relocation of coastal populations would create havoc at levels beyond comprehension. Added to the burden of looking after a displaced population is the burden it would put on natural resources. Imagine a city like Delhi having to accommodate an influx of people from coastal areas. A city reeling under the scourge of jammed roads, water shortage, power shortage and law and order problems would crumble at the very outset! Imagine what would happen to other cities which have fewer resources than the capital city!

Can we, therefore, afford to sit back relaxed in our living rooms watching happenings taking place in faraway places like

Tuvalu, or Mauritius or Seychelles or even a little-known village called kivalina? The answer is a clear no! We all need to get our act together and Governments need to work towards fighting the common cause of Global Warming. Developed countries need to contribute more towards the fight to contain Global Warming, both in terms of financial support to the developing countries for the introduction of green technology and in terms of a sincere intent of doing more to protect the world from a crisis! In a world that is energy hungry, dependence on crude oil and the resulting impact on the environment are the main culprits for global warming. Global warming in return is the result of a very sick environment! Someone once told me that the measure of a country's economic powers lies in the amount of crude oil consumed by it. This is something that we need to change. An immediate reduction of dependence on crude oil, research in alternative energy sources and popularization of a green philosophy of life can perhaps stem the uncontrolled descent into a chaotic situation! Indian has been largely impacted by global warming. We have witnessed an increase n the occurrence of natural disasters caused by global warming. The recent cloud burst that took place in Uttarakhand resulting in a destructive deluge has caused massive destruction to life and property. While no doubt it was caused by nature, one can never ignore the fact that massive deforestation coupled with building of hydroelectric power stations, building on river beds, and overexploitation of natural resources might have exacerbated the situation. It has been known that global warming has been responsible for excessive melting of glaciers in the Himalayan mountains. This has resulted in a series of flash flood resulting in immense loss to life and property. Global Warming is not a Myth, it is a Reality; many would argue that global warming has always been around, and there is no way we can doubt this. A better and more effective term would be, Climate Change. While few will argue against the claim that human industrial activity is indeed one of the reasons for frequent shifts in weather patterns which includes rainfall patterns, perceptible shifting of seasons and so on.

PASSAGES

One of the indicators of a shift in seasons is the shortening of the winters as compared to the lengthening of summer seasons in India. June and July used to be two months where there would be heavy rainfall, and by September the weather would mellow down so that it became pleasant in September. Today, after a period of twenty five years one can see how the rainfalls have failed, and winters have become short.

Questions on comprehension

A. Answer the following questions according to the given passage:

1. What is threatening the existence of Kavilina village?
2. What does the writer mean by saying, "We still have borrowed time?"
3. Where is Kiribati island situated? What threatens this island? What is the alternate settlement?
4. Why are Maladives, Mauritius and Seychelles popular? What is threatening them?
5. What are the factors which make the Indian coasts highly vulnerable to this threat?
6. What does global impact of rehabilitating population mean?
7. Justify the line – "Global warming is not a Myth."
8. What does the writer mean by saying 'Shift in seasons'.

B. Find the antonyms of the given words from the passage.

1. afforestation
2. liable to stand firm
3. shoot up from water
4. unknown
5. Forzen
6. Pure
7. Orderly
8. Can't be seen

C. Find the synonyms of the given words from the passage

1. like a story
2. not refined
3. with purpose
4. place to which someone belongs to
5. impure or diseased
6. fear of getting extinct
7. Springing back
8. Feeling of self satisfaction
9. To move unsteadily
10. Prevent the use of
11. To take to another place
12. Can be seen

IS DIGITAL EQUITY A REALITY?

Digital Equity is an elusive Civil Right even today, thus it is a major issue that can be put to the debate. People believe that technology should provide everyone with opportunities for growth. However, the reality is that although we might thrust Digital Technology onto the entire population of a country, the fact remains that a large number is still Digital Technology Illiterate! Some don't even have an access to Technology. It is clear that Digital Equity is a major issue that divides the society into the haves and the have nots! Those who have access to Digital Technology might get the best jobs or even get admission to some of the best colleges without being really intelligent or even accomplished professionals, while those who really deserve to get that seat because of their abilities are left out just because they don't have that internet connection or even a Smartphone!.

It is an unfortunate reality that lack of Digital Equity and thereof the lack of opportunities for all have resulted in a society that is in a state of a divide. Take for example the tedious process of registering yourself for a seat in a college. Unless you are tech-savvy, it is going to be difficult for you to get yourself registered. A large number of students aspiring for a seat in a prestigious college in the capital city might be left out for the specific reason that they don't have a good internet supply in the countryside, or perhaps their internet device is not capable of handling the pages on the college website. A few students might outsource the filling in of their college forms to the Guy running the Neighbourhood

Cybercafé, in many cases for an exorbitant amount! Where then, is Digital Equity?

A large number of people living in the country are the elderly, those who have somehow managed to handle cell phones that have a keypad, they might have tried a smartphone but are nervous about using the touchscreen. With the Government insisting on Digital Payments, the elderly are simply at a loss because they don't know how to use the technology. The fact of the matter is that Technology has become for some, a monster that refuses to let go!

Most of the jobs today require some kind of basic skills in handling computers. Some people can't imagine that there are a lot of people in this world who are simply not computer literate. Would you expect a Janitor to be able to fill in an excel sheet or even share his schedule on a Google sheet?

So then, can we in any way claim that Digital Equity exists in our world today? Can we claim that everyone on this planet has access to electricity, technology and an internet connection that is reliable? In a world that reels under shortages of power, water, basic resources, can we turn a blind eye towards those who don't have access to digital technology and expect them to compete with those who have access to the same? How much does being Tech Savvy make you a better person than one who is not? Has technology helped you improve your scores on a test? Has it made your handwriting better? Does being Tech Savvy give you the right to the coveted seat in a world that is unfair in the opportunities it gives to all its citizens?

It all boils down to the dichotomy between intellect and Tech. Savviness. Being Tech Savvy does not necessarily make you an intellectual, in the same way, that being an intellectual simply does not make you Tech Savvy! Both of these skills do not always connect!

What is badly wrong about our understanding of Digital Technology is that we have a seriously flawed idea that access to Digital Technology (and being Tech. Savvy) automatically makes us better than others! The fact is that Digital Equity is still a distant reality, and at the most a misnomer, all illusion that we are deluding ourselves with!

Questions on comprehension

A. Answer the following questions according to the given passage:

1. What do people believe? Why are the words 'Digital Technology illiterate" Used?
2. Why is Digital Equity a major issue that divides the society?
3. Why has it become a nightmare to fill up admission forms to take admission in colleges?
4. Why have digital payments made some people so nervous specially when the transaction is through government for admissions?
5. What are the reasons which keep the intellectuals in the back seat?
6. Whose future is bright? Why? Can this watershed be leveled easily without taking much time?
7. Explain the expression 'haves and have nots'.

B. Find the synonyms for the following words from the passage.

1. with little or no education
2. right judgement
3. expert in one's undertaking
4. push suddenly
7. situation
8. special
9. Keenly desired
10. Gate keeper taking care of a building

5. having merit
6. truth which is unlucky and can't live without it.
11. Ignore
12. Deceiving

C. Find the antonyms of the given words from the passage

1. incomplete
2. exciting
3. without reputation
4. literate
5. unimportant
6. avoiding
7. Weak to over power
8. Can't be depended upon
9. undesirable
10. Right opinion

A DUSTY AIRPORT

It was rather an unassuming Airport in nineteen seventies, nothing more than a dirty dirt – track that served as a runway with a wind sock and a radio antenna that was raised on a pole. Samson, my classmate in class seventh and eight was the airport manager's son and he would often take me to the airstrip to give me a tour of the planes that landed there. In those days the aircraft that frequented the airstrip were the Dakotas, a double winged Canvas Tiger Moth aircraft that served as a crop sprayer, and a few single engine aircraft that seated six passengers and had the legend Admass Air emblazoned on the sides. In those days all communication between the pilot and the airport was via the short wave radio which could be heard on ordinary radio sets!

Of all the aircraft that landed and took off from the airstrip, the D.C3 was the most impressive ! Just before the aircraft landed, the pilot would call up the Airport Manager, the airstrip would be cleared of the animals grazing around the airstrip and the D.C. 3 would touch the edge of the airstrip trailing behind it rather a long stream of dust behind it. The D.C3 squatted on its tail with a nose up attitude after landing which seemed to be rather strange because when parked, the D.C3 had a nose pointing up towards the blue sky. Samson often took men on a tour of the plane and it felt rather odd, walking up an incline from the tail towards the cockpit. This plane also had a tiny chemical W.C. at the tail. My memory of flying in this plane goes back a further few years when at the age of three or four we flew from Mekele to Asmara. It was a most eventful flight (except for the tendency of the plane to drop a few feet each time it hit an air pocket) and there were only four of us, both my parents, my brother and I in the whole plane!.

This D.C3 had never flown at a very high altitude. In those days, the pilots usually followed the terrain relying on their compasses only from time to time. The plane had seats that could be folded over to make space for the cargo. I often observed that besides sundry parcels, odds and ends, the aircraft was loaded with corn. The only time I was aware of an accident, the D.C3 couldn't fly over some tree tops. All we knew that two young pilots had lost their lives.

The wreckage of the whole plane could be seen from the main road just a few kilometers from the highway that led out of the town. I remember the crash site with my father and brother. The place had cables, instrument panels and melted blobs of aluminum littered all over.

Questions on comprehension

A. Answer the following questions according to the given passage:

1. Why is the Arbaminch airport considered to be unassuming?
2. Who is Samson? What role did he play?
3. Why did the landing of D.C3 look strange to the author?
4. Who were the passengers that travelled from Mekele to Asmara? Why was it an eventful flight?
5. Where did the D.C3 crash? What were the reasons? What littered at the place of accident?

B. Find the synonyms for the following words from the passage.

1. Various small items
2. discarded things lying here and there
3. track for a plane to take off
4. turning to do something

PASSAGES

5. sit on one's heels
6. goods carried in a Dakota
7. ruins
8. Come down to stand still

C. Find the antonyms of the given words from the passage

1. unnoticed
2. considered as true
3. machine used to give out perfume to feel good
4. not leaving good impression
5. familiar
6. forgetful
7. Height from the ground

MONEY PLANT

My brother-in-law and I spied a money plant creeper crawling on
A wall, with leaves so big, and darkest green in colour, larger than
Life ! And we were filled with greed so to steal one strand to plant
At home and watch it flourish and grow !

So, the next day we took a knife hidden in a roll of paper on our
Morning walk, and when no one was looking, stepped with care,
And cut off one strand of the robust bright green money plant !
We carried our prize with great pride to watch it grow.

One strand I took with me to plant at mine own home, the other
One I gave to my brother-in-law. But alas! His did wither away,
While mine did languish and shrink till all that remained
Was a rotten stub poking from the pot!.

And I wept to see how this robust plant had withered away
In spite of all the care I had lavished on it; for to be away
From its brothers and sisters had robbed it of all its will
To live, so I left it, though I watered it oft !

Then one day did I see a bright green leaf poking, from the
Rotten stub, and then another, and another, and then Lo,
Behold a tiny green plant emerged from the rotten stub,
Full of life reaching out to the sky above !

So do I salute the spirit of survival in a plant separated
From its kith and kin, that from the almost dead emerged,
One so robust, A testimony to the spirit of survival,
A lesson for the weak, "If a plant can emerge from a
dead stub, can't you from a life of defeat?"

Questions on comprehension

A. What do the given verses mean?

1. 'Darkest green colour, larger than life !'
2. 'We carried our prize with great pride !'
3. 'His did wither away ! While mine did languish and shrink'. Whose plant had died and what happened to the poet's plant?
4. 'Stub poking from the pot'.
5. 'And I wept', why?
6. 'Robbed it of all its will'
7. 'One day I see' – what did the poet see?
8. 'Full of life' – what was full of life? Why?
9. What does the poet 'salute'?
10. What is the testimony to the spirit of survival?
11. What is the lesson for the weak?

B. Give synonyms for the following words according to the poem?

1. like thread
2. continuing to live
3. move slowly on ground
4. vigorous
8. Knowledge of one's worth
9. decayed
10. Lack of life
11. Generously

5. to become dry, faded
6. appear
7. to overcome
12. Make a hole by pushing something
13. Grow in a healthy manner
14. Declaring

C. Match the antonyms with the words given in the poem.

1. hurrah
2. look for something openly
3. become tight or small
4. large
5. brightest
6. Welcoming an officer by turning one's back
7. Together
8. Enemies
9. Openly
10. Strong
11. Without desire
12. Unattentive

A TRAVELER OF LIFE

Yes, I am a traveler of life,
And the journey is long; the twists and turns are many,
And the road never so plain. The ups and downs are heady,
But they promise an eventful journey !

Many a roadside scenes have I seen:
A group of noisy children, grubby but keen!
A couple of geese waddling across the road.
Yes, I am a traveler of life and have seen it all!

The addict stands in the centre of a road, directs
Traffic with verve and swerve, unafraid, as
Monsters, roaring, bear on him! And sure,
Have I seen it all for I am a traveler of life!

I see a couple of girls giggle over ice-cream
While two children sleep on mats next to them,
Two children whose parents sell fruits on a cart.
Yes, have I seen it all on my travels of life.

So does my journey speak of sweets and bitters
Sours and hot, all in a single morsels!
I have seen the innocent smiles of a child
And the tears of the destitute sitting by the road !

Yes, I'm a traveler of life,
And sure, have I seen it all – the twists
And Kinks, dips and rises eventful
Like a river that flows down a hill!
The weeping of the aggrieved, and the laughter
Of the happy, the anticipation of victory,
And the fear of impending defeat – two faces
Of a coin, that promises a journey eventful enough!

Questions on comprehension

A. Explain the given lines.

1. Why has the poet said, "The road never so plain?"
2. What do 'ups and downs' signify? What do they promise?
3. What has the poet seen on the roadside? Why are the children so keen?
4. How does the addict direct the traffic?
5. What is the danger, the addict is unafraid of?
6. What is the mood of the girls?
7. What are the two children doing? Whose children are they?
8. What kind of eatables are available?
9. What is the mental condition of the destitute? Why do you feel so?
10. What is being called eventful?
11. What figure of speech has been used? Explain it
12. Why are people weeping and others are happy? What is their anticipation?
13. What does the poet mean by saying – two faces of a coin?
14. What makes the journey eventful?

POEMS

15. What is the refrain given in the poem? What does it emphasis?

B. Give synonyms for the following words according to the poem?

1. expected
2. twist in the length of a wire
3. headstrong
4. nthusiastic
5. soiled, dirty
6. tiny piece of food
7. laugh in a silly way
8. without food clothes and necessities
9. Important happening
10. Kind of birds
11. Walk with slow steps and sideways
12. Huge, and misshaped
13. loud sound
14. Full of sorrow
15. About to happen
16. Failure

C. Give antonyms according to the words given in the poem.

1. cold
2. carry or borne
3. not certain
4. tastes like lemon
5. Goes down
6. Feared or being afraid
7. Taste like a ripe sweet mango
8. straight
9. failure

TO KISS THE STARS

If I could slow down time and beat the stars at their game, I'd
Be the brightest one in the sky ! To hold time by her hand
Would please me ! so grab hold of the moment before it slips
Away, and plants a kiss square on her lips or she slips away.

You get only one chance and 'proof', it's gone before you know,
Leaving you to live a life of regret so great, so grab hold oh,
The moment, dear, and plant a kiss, on her lips before she
Turns away, 'would be my advice to all those friends out there !

As life goes by, a never ending stream, you sit by the shore,
Attempting to arrest some of the waters that flow through your
Finger! But life being so ever changing, so never the same.
Grab hold her hand and kiss her on the lips before she goes!

Thus do lovers sere and sad, wreck their hearts and livers;
As they lament a moment lost, with panting signs and ears
That twitch, for a sound of beloved's returning feet. But, Alas!
Has the moment passed, and they are left twiddling their
thumbs!

Read the following lines and answer the given questions

1. If I could slow down time and beat the stars at their game, I'd
   Be the brightest one in the sky! To hold the time by her hand
   Would please me!

- a. What does the poet want to do? Give your answer in two sentences.
- b. What does he want to become?
- c. What would please him?

2. So grab hold of the moment before it slips
   Away, and plant a kiss square on her lips ere she slips away.
   - a. Why has the poet used the word 'slips' twice?
   - b. What should a person do to hold the time back?
   - c. What literary device has been used?

3. You get only one chance and 'proof' it's gone before you know, Leaving you to live a life of regret so great, so grab hold oh.
   - a. What does the word 'chance' stand for?
   - b. Why has the word 'regret' used?
   - c. What is the advice? Who has given the advice?

4. As life goes by a never ending stream, you sit by the shore, attempting to arrest some of the waters that flow through your Fingers ! But life being so ever changing, so never the same,
   - a. How is the life connected with a stream?
   - b. What does a man attempt to arrest? Why?
   - c. Why is life called ever changing, never the same?
   - d. Give literary device

FREEDOM

Freedom, you are an elusive bird,
You tell me that freedom means,
The right to express myself !
The right to sing loudly,
To move wherever I wish freely,
Without fear !

Freedom, you don't mean license,
But to respect others, to choose,
What will be best for me,
That I should be what I be,
Dear Pa, I want to be a rock-star!

Freedom, you mean release from
Fear that I might stand before,
You without trembling ! to be
What I meant to be, a flame
To ignite young minds to be
What they will be, a bright star in the sky!

Freedom, you free me from
The shackles of slavery, from
Traditions, customs and ritual, and superstitions,
That I might be different from you !
I will be what I want to be !

Freedom, you guide me to the stars,
Of thought and new ideas and dreams,
That I might strive to be what
I wish to be ! you tell me best,
That I might be what I can be,
An engineer, or a teacher to lead others!
Freedom you free me from fear,
To speak my mind, and sing to my heart's elation
And go where I like ! You give me joy to live,
Not as a slave to custom and tradition, but
A maker of mine own rules, customs and destiny !
I will be a drummer or a singer!

Freedom you are surely an elusive fairy,
To guide me through immense possibilities, to
Invent what I want, to travel back in time,
To view the future, of what the world might be!
You have caught me that I am the maker
Of mine own destiny, and fate

Questions on comprehension

A.

1. Why has the poet called 'freedom;' elusive bird?
2. According to freedom what does it signify?
3. What poetic device is used in the first stanza?
4. Explain the given verses – Freedom, you don't mean license, but to respect others, to choose
5. What has the poet chosen?
6. What shackles are there from which the poet wants freedom?

7. What do stars refer to?
8. What does the poet mean by, "my heart's elation"?
9. Why has the poet called freedom "an elusive fairy? What is the poetic device? "Freedom you are surely an elusive fairy"
10. Why does the poet want 'to travel back in time'?
11. 'I am the maker of mine own destiny, and fate." Explain.

B. Give antonyms for the words given in the poem?

1. softly, in low voice
2. disrespect
3. freedom
4. not afraid
5. boredom
6. Not allowed
7. Being eligible to do something
8. Strong desire

C. Give synonyms for the words given in the poem.

1. belief in magic
2. to increase enthusiasm
3. tending to escape
4. written permission to do or use
5. prevent freedom from doing something
6. Belief carried from generation
7. Make free
8. Shake involuntarily
9. Continue the activity something
10. Many
11. happenings which are likely
12. discover

www.ingramcontent.com/pod-product-compliance
Lightning Source LLC
Chambersburg PA
CBHW071736150426
43191CB00010B/1589